M000196769

SIGNPOSTS
HELL, HEAVEN AND HERE

TINA BLACKWELL

Star House
PUBLISHING

Signposts
Hell, Heaven and Here

© 2019 Tina Blackwell

Edited by Lisa Rapp

Published by Star House Publishing

For any information regarding permission contact
info@starhousepublishing.com
www.starhousepublishing.com

ISBN 9781989535066

Printed in the United States of America
First publication, 2019.

Cover design and typesetting: Amir Saarony

For Mom

You never left my side and made me get back up
every single time.

This book would not exist without you since there
is no doubt I would have been gone long ago.

I love you a million pumpkin pies.

You are, have always been and will always be my Signpost.

Kent MacLeod, the man who singlehandedly brought me
back to life. Thank you for writing *Biology of the Brain*.
This book will not only enlighten doctors around the world
in truly helping their patients, but empower everyone dealing
with a disease.

Honestly Kent, you are exceptional for taking on this
endeavour. The science in this book will save countless
others from having to endure such a journey as mine and
will actually prevent illnesses and diseases to begin with.
www.BiologyoftheBrain.com

Foreword

by Bentinho Massaro

I met the author for the first time on stage in front of 200 people. Having been a spiritual teacher for about a decade, I have had many people come up to me to tell me all kinds of unusual (and oftentimes partially or wholly delusional) stories or claims about themselves, about me, or about their connection to me. I will spare you examples, but suffice it to say, the things you hear in my field of work or as a public figure in general, aren't always pretty, sane, or grounded in any objective sense of a consensus reality.

So when Tina walked up to the stage after being picked from those who raised their hand to come up and ask a question, I noticed another potential for "crazy on stage" was approaching. As she sat down in the guest chair next to me in front of the large audience, she stared at me intensely—also not uncommon in my position, as "eye gazing" is a big thing for some spiritual seekers. She then shared something that would be hard to believe for most people. She describes this herself later on in her book, so I won't spoil it here.

Although I'm sure the statement Tina made in front of so many people sounded delusional to some even in that crowd, there was nothing in her vibe that felt needy, weird, overly dramatic, sexual, manipulative, self-obsessed, delusional or otherwise ungrounded. So, as I waited for that recognizable feeling of, "Here's another sweet soul who's lost the plot a bit..." to arise—as had been the case with many who came before her—the feeling of "crazy" never hit me. Instead, I could feel that this woman had lived through something very real, which had resulted in a state of confidence that nobody could take away from her, no matter what they said, believed or critiqued her for.

There was something solid and humane, loving and compassionate about her. She seemed able to truly pay attention to another human being; to know what is being communicated at the heart, and to see through the bullshit surrounding it. She radiated a high level of genuineness, which is something I think is quite rare in humans, mainly due to our obsession with comfort and safety, often at the expense of joy, truth, inspiration, risk, generosity, service-to-others and dedication to something greater or deeper than just our personal circumstances.

I could sense this woman was beyond caring about her comfort or safety. She was present.

It was quite clear to me, even during that first meeting, that Tina had been through one or more "hero's journeys" and that life's natural intelligence had "sobered her up" and smacked the basic egotism and victimhood we are all raised with out of her system. This had made her a real and truly available human being.

I could tell she was here to own the truth of her experience and use it to make a difference in other people's lives; she wasn't interested in just securing more stuff or ideas for her comfort or self-image. She was fierce, generous, ready and awake. Fit for duty.

When Tina asked me to write the Foreword, it felt like a perfect reflection of the nature of our connection. I felt honored. However, I also felt a slight reluctance to actually read the book, because I knew I would be in for a ride. Being as empathic as I have developed myself to become through my "profession ," I can feel the details of anything I imagine as if it's happening to me directly. This happens mainly because I know that, in truth, it is happening to me, for oneness is not a mere concept to one who has realized its reality. This effectively means that whatever I put my attention on acts as a keyhole into a vivid experience of an alternate version or extension of my Self. In this case, Tina's life.

As it turns out, pretty much everything described in the book was information she had never told me before! This, I feel, is another testament of Tina's genuine intent: she is not carrying her suffering around on a platter for all to see. She's not deriving "bragging rights" from everything she went through. She did not write this book to have the world recognize her pain, perseverance and transformation. She wrote this book because her heart has been broken open by a little thing called "life" and this has ignited within her a much greater love and awareness of others. Through this awakened heart, I believe she sees the heart of the collective much more clearly, as well as its cries for clarity, love, guidance and courage. She consequently desired to share with others her remarkable story in the hopes that it may provide them with a little of just that. And I believe it can.

I finished reading through the book in two nights back-to-back. I read from approximately 11:00 p.m. until 6:00 a.m. on both nights while I was rested in a lounge chair greeted by the starry night sky over a large private property in India. It was the perfect timing and the perfect place to read this story. The whole experience left me feeling "energetically cleansed" of some ever-so-subtle complaints about my life that lingered in my nervous system like a string of invisible and unintended psychic hitchhikers. I'm generally in a very clear space of body, mind and spirit, yet Tina's book left me feeling deeply cleansed and replenished.

I believe that story-based media, such as books and films, provide us with the opportunity to learn from experiences without having to endure the actual catalyzing scenarios first-hand. Films and books are fantastic tools that can help us extract the lessons—at least to the degree we are willing to consider such lessons—from many different challenging situations in life, without having to attract or create the physical manifestations which generally inspire such life lessons.

The movies and books that have the most impact on us are never the merely distracting or purely entertaining stories, but rather those that put us in someone else's shoes in such a way that it feels like we went through the same journey for a few hours, yet with our physical comfort largely intact. In this way, we can learn from others' lives with only a fraction of the cost inflicted upon our own daily lives.

What a sweet way to be able to expand our horizons, increase our understanding of ourselves and each other, deepen our compassion and maturity as human beings, and finally accelerate our personal, inter-personal and spiritual growth—by simply paying for a book or a movie, rather than paying for such lessons with years of ongoing pain and struggle. What a gift, when used intentionally.

The principle of "downloading and uploading learning experiences at a fraction of the cost" is the same from your end toward other-selves. Take your own life for example: I believe you have chosen a series of challenges for yourself with the intent to arrive at a series of beautiful revelations and resolutions in this lifetime. I believe you have chosen a precious life theme to explore in this incarnation which—once you embrace it and learn to intentionally interact with it—will become your greatest source of power, learning, inspiration, growth, independence and even liberation.

The way I see it, we are all in this together. Whoever you are, you are partaking in this canvas of infinite exploration. I love you for everything you are and for all of the unrecognized challenges you choose to carry—not only for yourself, but for the Creator and for all the seeming other-selves that are part of this magnificent Creation. So truly, thank you for your bravery. I believe that together we are gradually untying the "karmic knot of the collective" as we each take a portion of this messy puzzle and transmute it through experience, patience, love, understanding and compassion. Perhaps finally one day, we will have undone all the knots that we have generated over generations of ignorance and succumbing to knee-jerk reactions.

And Holy Cow. Jeez Louise. Prepare yourselves! This particular piece of the puzzle you are about to read—this real life story, regardless of how you choose to interpret it–will inevitably take you for a ride and leave you with a fundamentally renewed perspective of your own piece of the puzzle!

This intense yet strangely magical story will flush out your mixed mindset and crystallize your priorities. It will help you strip everything that's not important from your life and your mind. It will show you what you are, what you are not, and where you are currently positioning yourself on the almost infinite line between these two points.

Something I want to emphasize is this: You can trust this book. It will not drop you or leave you in agony. It is intense and may put you face to face with some fears you'd rather not consider, but Tina's personal writing makes it OK, and the beauty of her approach makes it a magnetic and overall pleasant read. This book will hold your hand until the very end.

This is a gift to yourself. It is a gift specifically designed for you, and it is no coincidence that you are reading this right now. Trust that. There is a signpost sitting right here in your very hands.

Even years from now, when the details of this story have faded into the recesses of your memory bank, the impact that this story will have on you can never be undone. There is your life before you read this book, and there is your life after you read this book, regardless of who you are or what you currently believe.

For some, the transformation will be subtle, but pervasive, and will continue to radiate its lessons as you live your day to day life. For others, the author's life story will create an immediate and undeniable fork in the road; the reader will be faced with a transformational choice to confront themselves right then and there. Even if the events in the book seemingly have nothing to do with the events in the reader's life, somehow Tina's story still radiates and translates directly into the reader's actual life.

Strangely, it never feels uncomfortable or imposing, because as much difficulty as Tina's story describes, it gives us wings in ways applicable to moving forward more courageously with our own life theme. Her story gives us a fresh pair of eyes. And sometimes, a fresh angle is all you need to dissolve every obstacle that is presented to you at that timing.

You see, Tina's story gives us perspective—and perspective will flood our systems with renewed energy and courage. What seemed solid and dense a minute ago, can suddenly seem non-existent. The obstacles we believe we're dealing with are often simply choices we're not aware we're making. Tina indirectly helps us become aware of the choices we are making and gives us a heightened opportunity to change or let go of what does not work for us any longer.

At certain moments, Tina's story blatantly makes the discomfort in your life, by comparison, look and feel like you are playing Pokemon on a Nintendo game console with your 5-year-old. It provides you with something to ponder and deeply consider: How would I respond if this was my story? Clearly it has happened to someone, and I'm sure it's happening in different ways to tens of thousands of people around the world at any given moment... so it's not a dismissible or unrealistic scenario. What can I learn from this? How would I handle this? Who would I become? What state of consciousness would I choose to commit myself to if I had nothing left to lose, or seemingly nothing to live for? Could I see the light in the darkest of days? How am I clinging to unnecessary definitions about my own journey that weigh me down? And quite frankly, how am I pretending to be weak and limited by using my perfectly blessed life as the main excuse to not feel happy and profoundly enabled?

In addition to being personally catalyzing to the reader, I cannot see how this book would not send every reader who completes it off into the world with a much deeper respect and compassion for every living creature.

There are always people we meet whom we don't mean to judge (and we don't feel we really want to), but it's as if we cannot help but carry a distaste for them. Somewhere along the way we picked up an idea—whether from our parents, the media, or a bad experience with a stranger on the streets—and we are now inclined to judge someone based on nothing but a vague trigger, smell, memory, sight, gender, color, language, political conviction, intellectual intelligence, or simple miscommunication. This then launches us all too easily into a knee-jerk type of illogical prejudice.

We judge before we even have time to think, let alone truly meet and be present to another where they are at. We drop the willingness to remember that we don't know shit about this person's life. We may even find ourselves judging ourselves for being judgmental and observe the absurdity of so blindly believing in the largely unfounded hypocrisy of our own biases.

If we want a more peaceful, loving world—which we desperately need to cultivate if you ask me—it is crucial that we deepen our commitment to unconditional love, or at least cultivate a powerful and activated compassionate understanding of ourselves and other-selves.

We just don't know what it's like to have the points of view, experiences, difficulties, upbringing, handicaps, fetishes, paranoias, dreams, hopes, beliefs, social circumstances and physical body that someone else has. We also don't know what their soul's mission and theme, or series of lessons for growth, is for this life and how it is meant to affect their predisposition or circumstances at any given moment. How intimately do we know anyone, truly? Even ourselves?

Tina's story will help you soften your prejudices, even if you don't know you're carrying such prejudices. The book will reveal some of them to you and carry them away for you, leaving you feeling more empty of bias and more open to love your neighbor as much as your own self. Speaking of which, this book will also deepen your love for your own self, which in turn, will aid you in loving your neighbor more deeply as yourself. For how can we love our neighbors as ourselves if we don't even love and understand ourselves?

This deeper love and compassion feels great. It feels true, pure, sobering, necessary and cleansing. Tina's story helps us grow up, right when we are tempted to believe we already have.

Tina's ability to conjure up this sense of compassion, maturity and empowerment in the reader feels remarkably natural and casual. Most importantly, in my opinion, she manages to do so without promoting the toxic trend of painting an unnecessary picture of an external perpetrator (or cause) and a victim (or effect). The compassion her account begets is one based on providing the reader with a more intimate understanding of what it must be like to walk (or not walk) in another's shoes. She is not promoting a compassion based on forced sympathy, pity, guilt, shoulds or fear.

I believe she does this naturally because she herself has come to understand that she is ultimately the sole creator and decider of her life's journey. She seems to understand that everything that happens to her is, in truth, happening through her for the sake of her growth as a soul, as well as for the purpose of improving her ability to make a difference in the lives of others. And so she willingly embraces, repeatedly, her piece of catalyst, which she has so honorably plucked from the ever-unraveling collective puzzle.

It is this perspective that I don't think I've ever seen blended so naturally and pervasively into what, from the ordinary 3D mind's point of view, is essentially a victim's story. What is so refreshing about this "victim story" is that it offers the reader an extreme example of the fact that what seems like a victim story can always and consistently be alchemized into a hero's journey—a journey imbued with true self-understanding, love, happiness, awakening and powerful service-to-others.

If we succumb to the victim mentality, we can all feel justified in endlessly saying that we are victims of life. If we bring it down to this level of entitlement, honestly tell me: who isn't a victim of life? But what's the point in playing the game that way? How is it helpful to you, to your children, to the planet, or to other human beings and future generations? If we allow ourselves and encourage others to succumb to this weakness—which is most certainly a current societal trend—I promise you there will be no end to our suffering as a species, and the destruction of our biosphere will be probable. In addition, there will be no end to the new damage and suffering we will inflict upon each other in the name of "empowerment," due to the unaddressed weakness caused by our belief in the perpetrator vs. victim mindset to begin with.

So let us take a stance together, first of all in the heart—energetically. Not against anyone else, but against the temptation of succumbing to the victim mentality. Let us transcend this temptation first, and then see what remains to actually be done, practically speaking, to balance out the playing field. Let's make sure our minds have dropped into the intelligence of the heart. For without that, my friends, there is truly nothing stopping us from repeating the last 25,000 years, filled with more than ten thousand wars—every single one of them fought in the name of some idea that seemed perfectly realistic and justified at the time. Ideas that we blindly believed, and for which we never consulted the reality around us or within us. We never asked the trees, the grass, the stars or the animal life to confirm that our ideas were the truth. Absolutely nothing in the true present moment of existence outside of the bubble of our minds ever confirmed these notions as real, valid, or necessary. We have fought over ten thousand wars because of our distortion toward believing in ideas with the conviction that the pictures projected into our minds by these ideas are based in reality or truth—when in fact, they are not.

Let us have a deeper and more willing look at where we are fed up with what seems to be life's bullshit, and turn it around to realize that this bullshit is not actually out there; it exists first and foremost within our own projections. When we realize this, we can heal our species and bring peace and true innovation to this world.

All too often in our world today, we eagerly mistake aggression for empowerment. Let me tell you something: True empowerment feels like you've been given a million-litre injection of total peace, healing, transcendence, understanding and brilliance from the deepest part of your being. It comes with a natural desire to aid in the transformation of this world, through powerful yet loving means and examples. True empowerment never feels like you're fighting someone outside of yourself. Never. If it does, even a little bit, it means you have not yet done the inner work required to acquire true empowerment. Instead, you're in an externalized shouting match with your own shadows, tearing the world apart while you believe you are acting in an empowered way.

This book helps the reader realize this error in a way that never gets too confrontational. It naturally makes you want to become a better master of your own self. And in that, this book adds its piece to helping generate world peace. Even though many of the topics I have touched upon in this Foreword are not directly addressed in the book, to me they are all indirectly implied, which makes it such a relevant story of patience, perseverance, humility and forgiveness—qualities that seem to me to be of utter importance to the present timing in human evolution, and dare I say, to our survival.

How much exactly this book cleanses your psychology and leaves you healed depends on how much you're willing to drop your ideas about yourself and about what's possible. But at least to some degree, it will reset you as a human being and deeply open your heart to forgive your own theme, and those involved in your story. And forgiveness, my friends, will change everything.

There is a magic in these pages. It is not there because of the literal words, but because of the space these words are soaked in. Trust the book. Be open to its many unseen messages; they may have been waiting for an opportunity like this to sneak through the crevices of your mind and wake up your sleepy spiritual heart.

May this story help you realize that all of your suffering is here to catalyze you into growth; that all hardship is here to destroy your ego and melt your mind into a river of love on its way to meet the Ocean of the Eternal Self-in-All through the unique, and at times jungle-like landscape, which is your life's unique theme.

With great appreciation for the reader's magnificent journey in the making, and with gratitude for Tina's willingness to embrace her extraordinary piece of the puzzle: I bless this book and its message and hope it will reach the hearts of billions.

Bentinho Massaro

Introduction

In Tina Blackwell's new book, *Signposts: Hell, Heaven and Here*, the reader is confronted with a perceptual shift that is not often embarked upon in modern life. All of us, without exception, are at one point or another "healing" from something. Life was never meant to be easy, but the rules of life are simple. All around us are "signposts" nudging us into exactly the direction that we need to be… right here right now.

Tina shares her personal journey in an eloquent and honest fashion without sparing us the immense challenges and hurdles that needed to be overcome to bring her to her greatest epiphany.

As a physician I am often confronted with questions of an existential nature: Why me… why now… why this? Events in our lives often happen when we least expect them. Is all of this simply coincidence or does the universe conspire for us, not against us, and we just do not realize it at the time? Life is a long journey and none of us knows where it will lead us… other than that we will all change form someday.

Tina is one of those rare people who has been able to take tragedy and turn it into growth. Her leaps of spiritual advancements throughout her journey can only be quantified as "quantum."

Of all the gifts she bestows upon us in her raw and very real work, the greatest of these is the power of forgiveness and acceptance in healing our bodies and minds, bringing us to who we really are—pure souls on an earthly journey. Through her own at times unbelievable series of life experiences, Tina opens the reader's mind to what is possible when we can learn to just "let go" and connect with who we really are, as opposed to wearing the "cloak of invincibility" that most of us navigate through modern-day life with.

There is nothing like serious illness or trauma to confront us with our finitude and put into question many of our long-held core beliefs and values. Tina sheds light on how her ability to question many long-held beliefs, and open herself to a completely new way of viewing things, led to her quasi "miraculous" healings.

Wayne Dyer once said, "Change the way you look at things and the things you look at change." Ms. Blackwell truly gives us a new lens from which to view tragic events in our lives and see them not as obstacles but as "signposts," or stepping stones, guiding us to exactly where we need to be. As Eckhart Tolle so eloquently stated, "You are where you need to be right now." Regardless of what happens to us in life, it is our perception of its meaning that makes an event either potentially traumatic or a growth experience.

The growth that is described in this book will inspire you to stop searching in all the wrong places… the answers have always been and will always be deep inside you.

I highly recommend this book for anyone who has experienced a serious injury or illness or who is going through challenging times. It is a wonderfully honest and beautifully written account of a very personal healing journey.

Markus Besemann CD B.Sc. MD FRCP©
Chief of physical medicine and rehabilitation
Canadian Forces Health Services.

Prologue

What is past is prologue.
~ William Shakespeare

There is no holding back in this book, as it was written in real time, as it happened and with all the gory details. "Life can be understood backwards; but must be lived forwards." Soren Kierkegaard. The same goes for this book.

I am all the writers in this book. I am Marie and I am Tina. I am also the guiding voice you will hear at the end of each chapter. I would love to elaborate further, but you're just going to have to take this journey with me, understanding this in greater detail as you read. All will be explained and understood in the end.

It will be shocking at times, and even heart-wrenching, but take my hand and go through this journey with me, trudging through the mud and the darkness. You will relate to where she was and hold on even tighter. You will learn and grow along the way, leading you to an expanded state of being with a knowing that everything is indeed possible. We will then walk into the light together, hand-in-hand.

PART ONE - DESCENT INTO HELL

CHAPTER ONE
Life Is Over — In an Instant

Marie had always been a firecracker, or so she'd been told, and always loved writing. Marie used writing not only as therapy for her brain, but also to keep a record of her life so that she could refer back to it when the memories escaped her, which they often did. This book exists thanks to those daily writings, for without them the details in this book would have been gone forever.

I would love to tell you all about Marie's childhood and life before the accident, as would she, but those memories have not returned. She has tried relentlessly to remember who she was, but unfortunately, she only has bits and pieces based on diaries, journal entries and stories people have told her. But there is one memory that never escaped her and that is of her first love, Kevin.

Kevin and Marie lived together when Marie was just sixteen. They were everything to each other, but since they were both too young to realize what they had, they let each other slip away. However, he was never far from her thoughts and always in her heart. Marie never stopped loving him, even though there was no hope of reconciliation. There were huge gaps in their relationship that she did not remember, but the love they shared was always front and center. How she longed for Kevin after life took a turn in the worst way.

Life as Marie knew it was over forever, and although she didn't know it at the time, it would be the greatest blessing of her entire life. I was always with her. I never left her, serving as a faithful guide. Although her journey would last almost twenty years, I knew at least a part of her was hearing me.

Marie had just completed a four-month placement with the Royal Canadian Mounted Police (RCMP) in Sudbury, Ontario where she was living. She had graduated from college and passed the recruitment tests. One of her biggest lifelong dreams—to become a federal police officer—was about to become a reality when everything changed in a nanosecond.

On a cold snowy day in 1996, Marie jumped in the car with her boyfriend Jake, for a four-hour drive that wouldn't last fifteen minutes. Sitting in the passenger seat that morning, never could she have imagined that soon thereafter, nothing would ever again be the same.

At an intersection not far from home, an oncoming vehicle turned in front of them, causing them to swerve in an attempt to avoid the collision, thus catapulting them over an icy snowbank and into a hydro pole. Due to the onset of shock, Marie was able to limp to the nearby police station and sit down, where she was then questioned. She has no memory of any of this, but I assume that her behavior and foggy answers instigated the call for the ambulance.

Her first memory is of waking up in the ambulance on a back-board, completely immobilized from head to toe, listening to the exaggerated sounds of the tires catching the icy snow banks. She had no understanding of where she was or why she couldn't move, which brought her much confusion and terror. A young medic, Dan, was carefully covering her with blankets and gently moving her hair from the multitude of straps holding her down. She remembers him fondly and could pick him out of a crowd today. His gaze was angelic and his presence reassuring. She loved Dan instantly, and something in his eyes told her she was going to be just fine... no matter what. Dan was soon out of focus as she faded away once again.

The sounds of loud voices, chaotic movements and beeping shook Marie from her slumber. She was assaulted by bright lights and surrounded by people in scrubs. She had to urinate so badly and kept repeating this need, but the answer was always the same: "Just go in your pants." This was unacceptable to her and she wasn't having it. She had saved up for two months to buy her Levis overalls and there was no way she was going to pee in them! Little did she realize that they were about to be cut off her, which would send her into a hysterical rage demanding that they reimburse her the $100 for which she had worked so hard. She was strapped to a backboard with a neck brace, completely immobilized and totally confused as to why, yet obsessed with her black Levis overalls. I sometimes wonder if shock is a safety mechanism of some sort… but one thing I know for sure—it is truly comical in hindsight.

Jake stood above her with his mom and sister. The look of horror on their faces haunted her that day and confused her even more, although she now had been told what had occurred. The excruciating pain in her body made her wince, and she was no stranger to physical pain after all the extreme fitness training she had done in preparation for the RCMP. What was wrong with her? Why couldn't she connect the dots? Why couldn't she make sense of any of this? She was so lost, but Dan's face and his soothing words kept popping into her mind and heart, filling her with such comfort, such warmth, that she couldn't help but feel safe and hopeful.

Since this is her story, I will let Marie tell you herself what happened on that fateful day and in the months and years that followed, but you'll hear my voice at the end of every chapter. I just know Marie heard me too.

Marie's Story

On the 12th of January in 1996, some person lacking a conscience caused my Mustang 5.0 to crash into a hydro pole at the approximate speed of 100 km/hour (60 mph). Although I only remember a few moments of it, the ambulance ride to the hospital was the most painful ride I had ever experienced. But there was Dan. I will never forget Dan or the words he spoke to me that day, nor the feeling of complete protection that filled my entire being. It made all the chaos vanish instantly as I drifted away into unconsciousness.

The other driver, a so-called "human being," had left the scene, and in spite of dozens of posters placed all over the city and in surrounding areas, as well as strong support and assistance from Crime Stoppers, he was never to be found or held accountable for his atrocious actions. Life as I knew it was over... forever. I was angry, venomous and so very sad.

Being a competitive gymnast for over thirteen years during my youth and in my college Corrections program, I had always been a very athletic person. In order to graduate, there were very specific physical fitness requirements, and I not only loved the challenge, but thrived on pushing my body to its limits. Ambition had never been lacking. Actually, the reverse was true: I often heard I was a firecracker lit at both ends. Putting myself through college while working as a bartender at night made graduating one of my proudest moments. My mom always preached that "if something is worth doing, it is worth doing well." The feeling of self-accomplishment was indescribable. I had done it and I had earned it, but now it was all for nothing. Everything I had worked so hard for—all of the sacrifices I had made to achieve my goals and make my dreams a reality—vanished like a cloud on a hot summer's day.

This unwanted and unappreciated life-altering accident left me completely dependent, having to rely on friends, family or any available physically-capable person for absolutely everything, from bathing to eating. I despised every second of it, especially the bathing. It was humiliating to have zero ability to do anything for myself. Helpless, immobile and on countless medications, I soon gained over fifty pounds, which just added to the soul-shattering shame.

My mom was aware of how much I needed her, and being seven hours away didn't stop her; she came to be with me as much as she possibly could. A weekend is very short, but she never once missed our two days together. She purchased an expensive wheelchair in her attempt to give me a little more confidence by allowing me to make an effort to get around my apartment and be somewhat more independent. She knew this forced dependency was killing my spirit; it was like being slowly but surely tortured by an invisible force. Little did she know that the sight of that wheelchair destroyed what little spirit I had left.

Mom wanted to call Kevin, but I adamantly shut her down. She knew Kevin was the answer but there was no way I was going to let him see me this way! I was overwhelmed and petrified. The pain was intolerable, brutal and overbearing. Never in my wildest dreams could I have fathomed that excruciating pain and a loss of independence could be this debilitating.

A few slow, agonizing months passed without change, and although I was taking insane amounts of pain medication, the pain persisted with a vengeance. The pain was like a conductor deciding at all times which music was played. I couldn't stand it; I was going crazy and I just couldn't live like this. I began physical therapy in the hope that it would provide some relief, encourage the leg muscles to support me, and help me regain some of the balance and coordination skills that I had lost. Since the accident, I had been completely unable to bear any weight on my right side, and being the stubborn girl that I was, I had fallen to the ground countless times. I hated the wheelchair. I wouldn't even call it *my* wheelchair because there was no way I was staying in that thing for the rest of my life—nor would I be seen in public until I was out of it.

With daily practice for eleven months, and with much assistance from the physiotherapists, my confidence was growing. This made walking with the braces much more comfortable, which was encouraging. However the pain remained consistent and unrelenting.

Once the physiotherapy concluded, I signed up for a pain management program. My mission to get my life back continued. I collaborated and experimented with chiropractors, homeopathic practitioners, countless doctors, massage therapists, acupuncturists, as well as my physiotherapists and kinesiologists—all to no avail. I was progressively getting worse and the excruciating pain would not let up, not even for a second. What the hell was it going to take? I hadn't been without a piercing headache since the day of the accident, and the migraines had become so severe and frequent that my mouth was full of painful sores from the associated vomiting.

A number of medical professionals were trying to help me. They were all in agreement as to diagnosis and treatment, but nothing was working. I was totally committed to getting better. I was working very hard, pushing myself to the absolute limit and really trying to stay positive. I was doing every single thing they were advising. I was taking every medication they prescribed. But regardless of how hard I tried, I was in torturous pain and I was repeatedly failing.

I was fully aware of the probable future damage to my body and of the horrible side effects of all these medications. But I was willing to pay the ultimate price, any price, for a lift out of this well of agony and frustration—with complete disregard for tomorrow. The pain was literally driving me insane and the humiliating issues with memory, focus, concentration and a complete inability to process information were just adding kindling to the fire raging inside. My life was unacceptable; this just could not continue. Something had to give, and soon.

I believe Jake felt responsible for my injuries since he was driving the car, and he became angrier by the day. He often told me that he should have just hit the truck, blocking the intersection, instead of swerving to avoid him, thus slamming my side of the car into the hydro pole. I am convinced that if we would have hit the unknown driver's vehicle head-on at that speed, we would have been killed instantly. What if I had been the only one killed? I wouldn't be going through all of this right now. What if the other person would have been killed and we would have survived? How would I have faced that? Why did this have to happen at all? I certainly never did anything to deserve this!

Jake had been a witness through it all, from the accident to the ambulance to everything thereafter. This was so very difficult for him because he knew and loved the pre-accident Marie, and there was no resemblance to her left. He had to sit by helplessly and watch the slow and agonizing deterioration of my physical and mental state, as well as the devastating emotional effects of the many failed efforts at trying to stop it. I wasn't the only one who suffered a great loss.

My doctor consistently increased my pain medication, but it was like dropping a handful of water into the ocean. I would sit in her office sobbing uncontrollably, begging her to take away the pain, even for a moment. She was at a loss and had no clue what to do, which left me feeling bad for her as well. She tried everything she could think of, yet nothing worked.

The frustration and hopelessness was too much to deal with and I became very depressed. I was so tired, but I couldn't sleep due to the severity of the pain. My brain still wasn't functioning correctly, so my mental processes were all mixed up. Therefore, confusion was a huge part of my daily life, and trying to keep my thoughts straight was an impossibility. There was also a nine or ten year period prior to the accident of which I had no recollection whatsoever. This just added to the uncertainty. I was so scared of what was to come. Why was I being so brutally punished?

Every trip to the pharmacy turned into a nightmare, as the pharmacists treated me like I was a desperate junkie, illegally trying to get more drugs. Regardless of how busy it was or who was within earshot, they would loudly announce, in a sarcastic and disgusted manner, that I was taking narcotics—even to the point of listing each one by name. "Humiliated" does not even come close to describing how I felt. I loathed the thought of having to get my prescriptions filled, never mind the treatment I was subjected to while I was there. I would literally obsess and panic, counting the days to the next necessary dispensing of my medications.

The pharmacists would also openly dispute my prescriptions, and due to my extreme confusion, I was unable to express myself properly in order to explain. I had no self-esteem or emotional control left. In tears, I would point to my doctor's telephone number and hobble away until they yelled out my name for pick up. I already felt like a total loser and their abuse certainly didn't help. If the refills happened to coincide with my mom's visits, she would go to the pharmacy to pick them up for me. Not once did they ask her a question or mistreat her. If they had, she would have knocked some sense into them in a hurry, and the old Marie would have done so as well. Never would they have treated the old me like that, ever. You can't imagine how frustrating this was for me. My mom and I couldn't understand their unconscionable, cruel and cowardly behavior.

But there was this voice, this familiar voice, that would break through the thoughts every once in a while…

"Marie , I've got you. You're not alone in this. There is nothing for you to worry about, beat yourself up over, or be frightened of. I will never let you fall. You are always safe, you are never alone and I love you more than words can say. I see you struggling against the current and swimming upstream—turn around and let the current carry you.

Why do you care so much about being seen in a wheelchair? What do you think it says about you that you need a wheelchair or arm braces? Why do you care about the opinions of others? You're seeing yourself as a loser, as a complete failure, and you're telling yourself this countless times a day. Why would you expect the outer world to reflect back to you anything different?

You are constantly judging yourself, but I'm here to tell you that you are perfect and whole. Never would you have tolerated such treatment prior to the accident, so why are you not only suffering it now, but treating yourself in the same manner? What has changed? Do you really believe that these limiting beliefs only became an issue due to these circumstances? Or did the accident bring them to the forefront so that they can be healed once and for all? Can you even glimpse that maybe this is a gift? Why are you looking for answers from everyone but yourself? The miracle you are so desperately seeking is already within you. You only have two choices in every moment—Yes or No!

Remember Dan, Marie? Remember him! He knows the way."

CHAPTER TWO
Insurance Torture

Constantly having to deal with the insurance company was really weighing on me. I just wasn't equipped to handle any of this, so I hired a lawyer. I wondered why I had waited so long and came to the foregone conclusion that I never dreamed I would be sick for this length of time. Not having to talk to my claim representative, whom I'll call "Ken" (a so-called "human being"), was a great relief. A couple of months went by when I received a notification on behalf of the insurance company regarding a disability assessment (DAC) that I had to attend. Not knowing what to expect, Jake accompanied me.

The doctor (and I use that term lightly) spent all of five minutes conversing with me. No examination of any type was performed at any time, and the x-rays I brought were not even removed from the manila envelope. The doctor then exited the small office, leaving Jake and I bewildered and confused. We both assumed that an examination and perusal of the x-rays would be done upon his return, or that perhaps this was just a preliminary meeting.

The nice-looking, well-dressed doctor returned shortly and sat down beside me, facing the door. As the words left his lips and penetrated my brain, I could not believe what I was hearing. I just had to be misunderstanding what he was saying! Or was this some kind of a cruel, sick practical joke? I realized it was real when I looked at Jake. He was sitting very quietly with an angry look on his face. I knew this look well. I was worried that Jake would lose his composure, since he wasn't very good at controlling his temper.

During our five-minute conversation with the doctor, we very clearly told him everything that was happening with my body, listing the injuries and describing the severity of my pain. I also detailed for him the life I so desperately wanted back, and that I would do absolutely anything and everything to get better. I had so many dreams left to fulfill and so much precious time had already been wasted. My only priority—the only thing that mattered to me—was getting my life back. At any cost.

This so-called "doctor" informed us that there was absolutely nothing wrong with me; that I was bright, outgoing, pretty and determined, and the precious and incredibly fulfilling life I so desperately longed for was mine for the taking. His advice was to just ignore the "little pains" and be positive; to live life to the fullest, exactly as I wished. And last but not least, he told me that I was the only one standing in the way of my dreams; that if I would just let go of the pain (which was all in my head) and put a little effort into it, all the physical, mental and emotional turmoil would disappear. Just like that.

I began to shake uncontrollably. Tears welled in my eyes and streamed down my face, soaking the envelope containing the x-rays that I was still holding. I couldn't speak. I couldn't think. My mind, as well as my heart, was racing as I stared at Jake, who got up and left the room. Unconsciously, I followed. I was in complete and utter shock. We were half-way down the corridor when I heard the doctor's voice call out, "You no longer need the braces!" as I hobbled along.

I was only 26 years old; using braces was not my choice. It was embarrassing and a constant reminder of how much I had lost. The gawks and stares I got were not pleasant; they were hurtful and damaging to my already shattered self-respect and sense of self-worth. Because of the physical aids I needed in order to walk, I refrained from going out in public unless I had absolutely no choice. Why the fuck would I use braces if I didn't need them? Was I starting a new trend or making a fashion statement? Did this doctor think I would *choose* to have this unnecessary stress and humiliation to add to my already pathetic life? In all honesty, my life was hideous, ludicrous and horrible.

As I turned to look at the doctor, he was gesturing with his arms to lift the braces off the floor shouting, "You don't need them! Just throw them away and walk!" As I was standing in the corridor watching him, I couldn't help but picture a third-rate television evangelist shouting, "Hallelujah!" to his audience, and a poor unfortunate actor miraculously standing up from his wheelchair crying and screaming, "I'm cured! It's a miracle—I can walk!" I so desperately wanted to change the channel.

I had to forcibly grab Jake's arm to make him leave with me. Looking back now, I should have let Jake go. Maybe that five-minute doctor would think twice before doing this again to someone who was so desperately in need of help. We drove home in complete silence, neither of us knowing what to say.

A few months prior to the disability assessment, my mom, with the best of intentions, had talked me into going to the mall to hang out and maybe even have a little fun. There she was, wheeling me around in a wheelchair, when we ran into an old roommate of mine. I could see the pity and disbelief in his eyes, even though he tried to hide it. I wanted to die. I was fat, disheveled and crippled.

I never again returned to the mall. I had worked tirelessly to learn how to walk with braces so I could get out of the wheelchair and get rid of the walker, only to be told by the five-minute doctor that I didn't need them after all? I guess I was just using them for fun?

Shortly after this event, Jake cracked from all the pressure and lost it. During a heated argument over something petty and ridiculous, he punched a hole in the wall right through to the spare room, missing my face by half an inch. Good thing I moved. My mom was livid and freaked right out on Jake. You should have seen her in action. At five-foot-three, in her nightgown, she had this six-foot-five man down on his knees, crying. Needless to say, she was not leaving without me. I spent the next couple of months with her and my godmother in London, Ontario, a few hours away.

With my brother's help, they dragged the truth out of me about my relationship with Jake. Since the accident, my sense of self-worth had been repeatedly shattered. My self-esteem was so low that I truly didn't believe I deserved any better. I was an invalid on all kinds of drugs, and I was incapable of making myself better. I was an all-time big, fat loser. How was I going to leave my abuser when I wanted to be punished? I was unworthy of love and I deserved to be punished.

My brother gave me strength and courage, reminding me of how special I was. He also reminded me of the relationship I had with my father, and that I didn't need to repeat it. I deserved love, and love doesn't hurt. With support from my mom, my godmother, my brother and his wife, I returned home. Jake was out of the apartment soon thereafter, and out of my life forever. I am not in the least saying it was easy; I went through a really hard time. But I had a lot of support.

Around this time, I received a letter from the insurance company informing me that I was being sent to a back institute for a physical capacity examination and assessment. I panicked. I was terrified, worried and unsure. Unfortunately, my doctor didn't put my mind at ease; she was not comfortable with this at all. After much consideration, I was able to assuage some of my fears, since this was a major back institute with a reputation to uphold. I was still dealing with the Jake situation, so I was trying to avoid any undue stress. But this wasn't just a person with a medical degree in a tiny office, this was a huge institute. I was soon looking forward to the appointment and was hopeful they would have some answers so I could finally get my life back.

The appointment finally arrived and I gave it my all. They informed me that in order to do a proper assessment, it was imperative that I push through and complete each exercise, regardless of the pain, since the calculations were based on the entirety of them. I was fully committed to getting better, so in order to get some help, I pushed through whatever they wanted me to do. I was more than willing.

By mid-morning, I was already exhausted and in severe pain. Having to stand for long periods without being able to lie down was devastating. I had been completely inactive since the accident; my muscles were weak and I had no stamina. I ignored the fatigue and the pain and kept doing what they told me to do—everything from pushing a grocery cart with weights in the basket, to doing consecutive sit-ups. Each exercise was causing tremendous pain, so I kept taking extra pain killers. After all this time, I knew what aggravated my physical symptoms and how to diminish them. But against my better judgment, I continued to numb the severity of the pain with more narcotics, and I pushed myself all the way through to the end of the day, completing every exercise.

Afterwards, there was no sense of achievement whatsoever, and I felt kind of disgusted with myself. In spite of my exaggerated efforts, I did not manage to accomplish very much at all. I lasted all day, but I did not last long with each exercise and I could not do many repetitions. In addition to the pain, I couldn't find the energy or the strength to keep going. The assessor's disapproving attitude and actions made me feel even worse. I felt ashamed of myself once again. I wasn't good at anything anymore; I couldn't even push a little bit of weight or do a few simple sit-ups. Another brutal reminder of what I had become... nothing!

By 7:00 p.m. that evening, my neck, upper back and collar bone muscles were completely seized-up; my shoulders were wrapped around my ears. All I could do was sob. The pain was so intense that it was intolerable, and I clenched my teeth in horror. I could not have imagined that this would be the result of a few simple exercises. Pain I expected; but spasms I just didn't understand. I would never have fought so hard to last the entire day had I known that this would be the outcome.

My friend Jen rushed me to Emergency and listed the medications I was on, since I was unable to stop sobbing long enough to speak. Ironically, the doctor on duty was the same physician who had cared for me the day of the accident and she remembered me well. She quickly injected morphine, and the relief was greatly appreciated.

Placing a metal brace on my neck, she proceeded to tell me that I had often crossed her mind and that she had wondered how I was doing. Her disappointment was obvious.

I felt so blessed that she was on duty that day and the one caring for me. It was comforting because she had been there that fateful day. Her sincere words and kindness provided more relief than the morphine itself, and were certainly a huge difference from the assessors at the back institute. I was being treated with warmth and compassion; what a wonderful and unexpected change.

This had to be a gift from Mémére and Pépére in heaven because it was exactly what I needed to restore my faith in people. The timing was perfect as well, since I don't think I could have coped with what was to come the following morning. With a second injection of morphine and the warmth in my heart from the doctor's incredibly supportive words, Jen finally brought me home and thankfully she spent the night.

It was one of the worst nights of my life, without even a moment of sleep. When the effects of the morphine wore off, I literally thought I was going to die. Actually, I was praying for God to take me. I kept screaming, "I'm begging you, God! Please put me out of my misery!" Jen was with me; thankfully I wasn't alone. But the pain did not cease—not even in the slightest.

In the morning, I called the back institute to explain what had happened. I told them in no uncertain terms that it was absolutely impossible for me to come in that day, and that we had to reschedule. They advised me that I had no choice but to complete the testing in its entirety; to attend and complete the day's activities. This was impossible. The most insignificant, minute form of movement caused intolerable pain. Even taking a breath made me wince. I couldn't understand their reasoning.

My doctor advised me to stay right where I was and she would fax them a letter. She was against this assessment from the beginning, so her distress was obvious. I relayed the message to the back institute, but they wouldn't hear of it, and they proceeded to forcefully and bluntly reaffirm their policy. Such blatant disregard for people with disabilities. How could they possibly expect a person suffering from multiple injuries and severe chronic pain to commit themselves to two full days of physical activity? Why wouldn't they reschedule?

Although my lawyer had advised me to follow the advice of the Emergency room and my own doctor's orders, I was so worried that I forced Jen to take me to the institute. I was convinced that once they saw the condition I was in, they would gladly reschedule. It was a dreadful ride; each bump was pure torture.

Heavily medicated and wearing my medieval-looking metal neck brace, I made my way to the reception area, assisted by Jen. The therapist immediately instructed me to go to his office and lie down. My condition was undeniable; my eyes were so swollen and red from crying that they were almost sealed shut. He walked into his office carrying ice packs and carefully unfastened the neck brace to apply the ice. For the next hour or so, I lay on the bed unable to stop sobbing long enough to describe my symptoms. Jen did her best to help. The therapist's eyes revealed compassion and remorse, but his words hadn't changed. Their policy would not bend for anyone, under any circumstances. He also explained the insurer's expectation—they had approved and paid for these two specifically designated days. Anything else was unacceptable and would result in an unchallengeable failure. I now completely understood that there were no compromises. I would participate or fail.

I again contacted my doctor to know what the worst possible outcome would be if I made the attempt to continue with the second day of testing, with the help of more pain medication. She was totally pissed off and did not mince her words. She ordered me to go home immediately. She could not believe I had gotten out of bed to go to the institute and that I had ignored her warnings. She stated that I had suffered enough, and that any physical activity could possibly result in serious and irreparable damage, if it hadn't already. We were definitely facing months of regression, but to what degree she could not say.

Terrified and in shock, Jen took my arm and brought me home. I told her to go, that her baby needed her, and I just wanted to be alone. I dropped to the floor of my living room and curled up with Judge, my Doberman. I must have cried myself to sleep, because I awoke freezing the next morning in the exact same place. I was unable to open my eyes. Why was this happening to me? I can't take anymore, I just can't. Please let it end.

I called my mom later that night. I broke down completely, telling her that I just wanted to die, that I couldn't live like this anymore. I could no longer find the strength to control my emotions or spare her the worry. She panicked of course, which was exactly the reason I had always held everything in and not shared it with her.

I desperately needed her and only her. She was with me seven hours later, and as I lay in her lap sobbing uncontrollably, I finally surrendered to my agony. Mom was devastated, to say the least, and knew exactly what needed to be done; there was no other way. She decided to leave her job and her life to move in with me. This is what made getting through this horribly trying time, especially what was yet to come, even possible. What had I ever done to deserve such a beautiful and incredible mom? I don't know, but I felt so very blessed, and still do.

The consequences of the back institute's testing were unbelievable, and this dreadful outcome could have been prevented. Had my doctor been able to state her concerns, refuse the insurer's physical capacity assessment, and disregard the threats made by none other than my claim representative, none of this would have happened. My mom wouldn't have been forced to give up her job and her life. And I wouldn't have been locked in a torture chamber with no escape.

It was only after the first day of testing, when the damage had already been done, that I came to know the power of regression... and now it was too late. It felt like the bones in the upper section of my spine, collar bone, shoulder blades and skull were being crushed from the swollen and spastic muscles, as if in a vice press. The pain was unbearable. I often lost consciousness, and Mom would helplessly watch over me until I came to again. This didn't have to happen. This was preventable.

After countless sleepless nights and full days spent lying down, along with too many pain and anti-inflammatory medications and consistent intervals of ice, I was finally regaining a little movement. I hadn't been able to do anything on my own, so Mom fed me, put pills in my mouth followed by water, gave me sponge baths, changed my pajamas (as well as my bed pan), and gently moved my legs and arms to keep the circulation going. She held my hair and the bucket while I threw up, then washed my face and brushed my teeth. She replaced my ice packs, wiped my tears, and lovingly cared for my every need without ever once complaining. She saved me from breaking even more than I already had.

After a while, I was finally able to return to physiotherapy, but I had to start all over again from the very beginning. Any progress I had made was non-evident. I was back in a wheelchair. And here again was this familiar voice telling me what I didn't want to hear...

"Marie, there is nothing wrong with you! You don't have to ignore the pain... you can fully surrender to it and redefine it, instead of resisting it and being tortured, which is causing you so much suffering. The life you are so desperately yearning for is already yours, and there is nothing stopping you but yourself. How can I show you that the physical identity you are so tightly latching onto has nothing to do with what you are? Neither does the mental capacity that used to come so easily to you. Let go, my girl, let go. Be aware of the judgments, the labels and the victim identity—these things are not you. It is just the movement of the ego and it is not personal. You are not suffering because of your circumstances, you are suffering because you are saying No to them and making them unacceptable. Just say Yes. Bring an inner Yes to this moment.

You are and always have been free. Love yourself unconditionally... no conditions, no conditions, no conditions. If you believe you deserve to be abused, then why be surprised at the abuse or blame the abuser? If that's what you expect, then how could it be any different? How do you expect anyone else to love you if you don't even love yourself? And how can you love another if you don't know how to love yourself?

You don't have anything to prove to anyone. If something doesn't resonate with you, then do not do it, regardless of the perceived consequences. If you're following your joy and doing only what resonates, then what possible consequences could ever matter?

Do you see your refection in your mom's eyes? She's your mirror, Marie; take a long look. Do you feel that? Her unwavering love, care and safety—do you feel it? That's what you are, what you've always been and what you'll always be.

I'm here and I've got this. Take my hand and just let go. I know you can hear me."

CHAPTER THREE
Would Suicide Be Better?

It was all for nothing. I had not needed ultrasound therapy for over seven months, yet here I was again doing ultrasound therapy. The equipment I used daily to try and repair, build and strengthen my injured muscles could not be used for another ten weeks. Yes, I was literally starting over.

Then I received the most disastrous news. I had always fully cooperated with the insurance company, even against my doctor's orders, risking my physical, mental and emotional well-being. To my complete dismay, they followed through with their threats, in spite of the fact that I had been to hell and back because of them. I was no longer entitled to income replacement benefits, and their decision was based on the findings of the five-minute doctor, as well as the back institute.

To say I felt devastated, desolated and panic-stricken doesn't even come close to what I was feeling. I could not imagine the grief and anxiety I was continuously causing my mom. She had given up everything for me and I had nothing to offer but anguish. I was the reason she left her employment, and now she was supposed to financially support me as well? How was that possible? I wanted so desperately to end my life in order to give hers back. I knew it would kill her if I went through with it, so I chose to continue living my pathetic life. But the thought of suicide haunted me.

There was absolutely no way I could work in my condition. Mom was receiving unemployment insurance, but it just wasn't enough. All of her savings had been spent on medical equipment and everything else I needed; there was nothing left. How were we supposed to live? Because there was no other way, I did something I swore I would never do—I contacted Social Services. Welfare. I, Marie, needed welfare. Me. What a feeling of lack of pride and dignity in that moment.

Despite my disabilities, which were obvious as I made my way into the office in a wheelchair, I was told I was not entitled to disability benefits. This was due to the insurance company and their reports. My reports were irrelevant. If I hadn't been completely upfront with them, explaining the entire situation, they never would have known about the insurance reports, and I would have easily qualified. In addition, they told me that any welfare I received would have to be paid back in full once the claim was settled. I was perplexed. Since when did Social Services become a loan institute? And wasn't their sole purpose for existing to help people in need?

Four weeks ago, after the assessment, if someone would have told me that my life would get worse, I would have called them crazy. It just wasn't possible. Or so I thought. After signing the loan papers from Social Services, I started receiving $465 a month. Borrowing money just to cover the bare necessities was unavoidable. Mom's credit cards and lines of credit were being maxed out one by one, so she kept acquiring additional avenues of credit.

My mom tried everything to remain positive, but I could see the worry in her face. Constantly having to stay strong, always picking up the pieces and being solely responsible for everything was taking a toll on her. She could see the overall deterioration in my well-being and she couldn't stand it. In sheer desperation, she decided to move us to a bigger city approximately six hours away called Ottawa, Ontario. There had to be someone in the capital of Canada who could help us find some answers.

She found us a little mobile home on the Quebec side of Ontario, where the rent was much cheaper. We had to borrow money regularly to cover the expense of the mandatory trips back to Sudbury every six weeks so I could continue under my doctor's care, since we were unable to find a new doctor in Ottawa willing to take my case. We also had to travel five hours or so in order for me to be examined by another specialist. Full-time employment for Mom was not an option; she had to drive and escort me to all of these out-of-town appointments. She continued to be my sole caregiver, as I was unable to care for myself.

The insurance company no longer covered rehabilitation costs. I was forced to stop going to physiotherapy, massage therapy, and chiropractic care. I must admit that I underestimated the value of these therapies, but it became very apparent once I stopped. My body seized up constantly, causing my shoulders to contract up to my ears. To take x-ray images of my neck, I had to hold multiple bottles filled with water in each hand to bring my shoulders down far enough to capture images of my upper spine. The migraines were constant and wouldn't let up. Mom did her best to massage me, trying to provide some relief, but it just wasn't helping. She would sit by helplessly and watch the endless bouts of pain and vomiting. The fracture in my hip socket made sitting unbearable, so I spent most of my time in a horizontal position.

We lived in a small uninsulated mobile home, but we had each other. We couldn't afford to fill the heating tank for the first couple of months of winter. It was cold, which certainly didn't help the pain. Mom was constantly covering me up with heating pads and piles of blankets. She tried her best to keep us fed, but all we could afford was Kraft dinners. I can't imagine how helpless she must have felt.

Mom sprang into to action once again and started cleaning people's homes. Let me say that fate had her pretty hand in this one! Mom heard from her friend's sister that someone down the road from our trailer was looking for a trustworthy cleaning lady. Immediately, Mom went to meet him, and of course he hired her on the spot.

After seeing the man with his nose buried in his computer for three months or so, she finally asked what he was doing. He replied that he was a doctor and was doing research. She was excited and immediately told him about me. Dr. L took me under his wing. I can't begin to describe how relieved I was and how much I appreciated this man. No more 12-hour return trips to the doctor every six weeks. And there was the possibility that just maybe he would have the answers I was looking for. Hope had returned!

Dr L understood how much pain I was in. He knew that sitting was torture, and that the noise in a busy waiting room would be overwhelming for me. So he always arranged my appointments at the very end of his day or at his home. He was an out-of-province doctor, as we were living in Quebec, so there were out-of-pocket costs that we couldn't pay. He personally took care of everything, since he knew we had no money. This lifted a huge burden off my mom.

He read all of my medical records, thoroughly examined me, sent me for all kinds of tests, and soon began injecting my neck, upper back, hip and leg with cortisone and analgesic anti-inflammatory medications. For very brief moments, I had my first glimpses of freedom from pain since the day of the accident. This brought relief and renewal of so much hope.

There are no words that can do this justice, as it has to be experienced to be understood, but suffering from chronic, unrelenting pain literally drives you crazy. I would pinch myself really hard on the arm or leg just to produce a different sensation, which I called a "sanity break." Visualize a dripping tap that has been rhythmically dripping for months, getting louder and louder by the day. You're on lockdown and there's no way you can get to the tap, since it's blocked by some invisible force. The effects of the injections were equivalent to someone periodically putting their hand underneath the drip. A sanity break.

At some point, I was diagnosed with clinical depression, which I wouldn't accept. Yes, the thoughts of killing myself were constant. I came up with vivid and detailed ways of doing it with little mess. And yes, I was sad and crying all the time. But I wasn't *crazy*.

Obviously, these were my uninformed assumptions of something I didn't understand.

I went through the embarrassment of having the antidepressant prescription filled and reluctantly took the medication. After a few weeks, I could not believe the change in my thoughts and emotions. Some of the clouds had finally parted. My thoughts weren't so dark, and the constant yearning for suicide wasn't as frequent and overpowering. More of my coping abilities returned, and living wasn't so unbearable. Whatever that stupid pill was, it was magic.

I was crushed to discover that the pill's effects were short-lived. There was one attempt after another to suppress the severity of the depression with additional medications and combinations thereof, all to no avail.

I was referred to a specialist at the end of 1997, the Chief of Physical Medicine and Rehabilitation at a big hospital on the Quebec side of town. After a few months, I finally had the privilege of meeting with Dr. B. Little did I know that this man would become my hero and change my life forever. He was unlike anyone I had ever met, and after numerous discussions, tests and examinations, Dr. B put my mind at ease by completely removing the stigma and shame regarding narcotics.

Dr B clarified the function of opioids in pain management and the science behind it, and described how the body builds tolerance to them. This explained why I was regularly requiring higher doses. He provided me with videos and informational packets to study. He also informed me that the short-acting medication I had been taking for over two years was insufficient to deal with chronic pain, especially after the length of time I'd been suffering.

The desired effect of Oxycocet only lasted a couple of hours, and due to the length of time I'd been taking it, my tolerance was very high. I was literally starving my pain and creating issues with "wind-up," which meant having to catch up to the unmanaged pain. It took more and more pills, as well as increased dosages, to achieve some relief.

This was exactly what had been happening since my accident. I wasn't a pill-popping drug addict! This was a roller coaster ride from hell. I would have some relief at the top, and I would desperately try to hold onto that relief at any cost. Then I would fall down the giant hills of excruciating pain. The fear and anxiety in anticipation of the upcoming valley is typical with chronic pain and short-acting medications. I wasn't a drug addict.

To have Dr. B treat me with such dignity and respect... there are no words. The judgment I had dealt with from countless people in the medical field, and from family members as well, had been too much to bear. Dr B recommended a new medication and turned his attention to the pharmacists. He explained that many pharmacists, as well as doctors, make assumptions due to desensitization, as well as not keeping up with continuing education.

He wrote a long letter to the pharmacist, explaining my condition and detailing how narcotics were mandatory for my treatment. He included pamphlets, videos, medical research and findings, all to be brought over to my pharmacy. By telephone he advised them that it was not only necessary, but imperative that they consistently upgrade their education, and that if they had been doing so, they would have completely understood and accepted the proven effects of treating chronic pain with narcotics. He also reminded them of the importance of treating everyone with compassion, respect and without judgment or preconceived notions. I was speechless. I wasn't a drug addict. He had taken such a weight off my shoulders, and this was just the beginning. He also wanted to have a discussion with a couple of my family members, although unfortunately this never happened.

Dr. B and Dr. L were now working together. My pain management program was completely overhauled by introducing a new medication called OxyContin, a time-released opioid. OxyContin slowly releases medication into the system over a 12-hour period at regular intervals. I was finally off the rollercoaster from hell, and my state of mind improved dramatically. Sleeping through the night hadn't been possible since the accident because of the constant interruption of the pain waking me every couple of hours. With this long-acting medication I was sleeping peacefully and feeling much better during the day.

I could soon feel my spirit re-emerging. I began volunteering at the YMCA, teaching the odd aerobics class. I was starting to be active again. It wasn't long before I was asked to join the YMCA team. I was actually working and earning my own money—what a privilege. I was so happy! I was back! The weight I had gained melted away. I was even on television and in the Ottawa Sun as the Sunshine Girl. I was on top of the world, making my family and myself very proud. I even started a relationship with a really awesome guy whom we'll call "Vincenzo."

Eventually, it all came crashing down. I was fooling everyone, including myself. I kept having to increase the pain medication to maintain this amazingly beautiful lifestyle that I didn't want to give up. I was doing something that I had always loved, I was supporting myself, and I was helping people. I pushed and pushed to the point where I was constantly running out of pain medication before it was due to be refilled. I was lying to everyone and in complete denial. Before every single aerobics class I would take a handful of pills just to get through the class. I continued this charade because I was a "somebody" again.

Dr. B and Dr. L gave me a dose of reality and I was forced to give up this charade or the inevitable outcome would be death. I was totally and completely devastated. I had let everyone down again, and I fell into an even deeper depression than I had experienced before. I was filled with self-loathing.

The antidepressants were increased and the OxyContin and Oxycocet were cut. I had to wear a Fentanyl patch until they were detoxed from my system. It was pure hell. I was convulsing, shivering, and sweating. The pain was so extreme that I even lost consciousness a few times. Mom and Vincenzo were so frantic that they brought me to a healer. I got through the detox, and finally, after a few days I was able to reintroduce my pain management regimen and start picking up the pieces.

I was ashamed of myself for letting it go that far, but I must admit I was also proud of the fact that I had even tried. I was so very thankful to my doctors for stopping the self-destruction before it was too late. No one was aware of the entire truth; not even me. I was in complete denial again. Dr. B realized that my doses needed to be increased much too frequently and he wasn't comfortable with this at all. He decided that it was time to lower my tolerance by using a different medication in an equivalent dose. He also advised me that this athletic lifestyle was way too much for a person with my disabilities and chronic pain. The cost was too high.

In May of 2001, Vincenzo and I were married. It was a huge wedding and my doubts were pervasive. I knew who this man had fallen in love with, and it was certainly not the woman he was marrying. Our wedding day was long and I was in severe pain, but I pushed on, hiding away in another room to cry every once in a while. I hoped we could find a way to make the marriage work, but somewhere deep inside me I knew it wouldn't. I had told Vincenzo and my mom that I left the YMCA due to a conflict with the manager. This was partially true, we certainly didn't see eye-to-eye, but this wasn't the reason. It was due to the consequences of my over-zealous attempt to return to my former life. No matter the cost.

I felt so much shame and guilt for all the lies and secrets that I finally told Mom and Vincenzo the truth about everything. I never wanted them to know that I was not physically capable of doing the job, and that I had gone to such extremes to hang on to that image. They both held me tight. Mom admitted that she had suspected it all along, due to the excuses I was making in order to get my medications filled early. She had been worried and was so relieved when I quit the fitness coordinator position. She loved me unconditionally and was immensely proud of me. Not because of a job title, aerobic champion status or some career, but because of who I am. My husband remained very quiet.

After some time had passed, Mom found me employment with the software company she worked for as a receptionist. Within a couple of months, I had taken over the entire marketing collateral fulfillment department and saved the company a ton of money.

Being back at work and productive again, I was feeling pretty good. I did have to increase my medication, but I was extremely cautious, following Dr. B's strict guidelines and honestly listening to my body's needs. I was quite successful at this job, and my bosses were noticing. I was given more and more responsibility and I was thriving.

A year went by quickly and my contract was up. The company was bought out and my department, which I had created from nothing, was moved to the new head office in Toronto. It had taken a lot of precious time, creative thinking and effort to create and implement the system I had developed, and I felt like they were stealing my baby. They did offer me a position, but not one I wanted or was even capable of doing.

A client of the software company heard that I was in need of employment, and I was soon offered a prestigious position almost identical to the one I lost, but on a larger scale. And the salary to go with it. They pulled out all the stops in getting me to accept their offer. They must have had very good resources since they sent me a beautiful vegetarian cookbook from my favorite restaurant, along with a basket full of goodies. I accepted their offer and started my new job immediately.

Again I underestimated my physical limitations, and within nine weeks, they relieved me of my duties. I was beyond devastated again. It took quite a while for me to figure out what had gone so wrong, since I had been so successful at my previous similar position.

After much pondering, I finally realized that I had no direct bosses at the software company I was previously working for; they were all in Toronto. I could work on my own schedule, around my flare-ups, and no one was the wiser. If it was a pain day and I needed to be in complete darkness and silence due to a migraine, I could stay home. Mom would take messages or transfer calls if I was able to communicate. I could work from home whenever I wanted, without distraction, and I had a fantastic assistant to handle any physical work. There was a cot in the room adjacent to my office, so I could lie down when needed. My work was impeccable and spoke for itself.

With this new job at the printing company, I was asked to attend all meetings, listen to everyone's ideas, suggestions and concerns, and find solutions as the coordinator. I never thought this would be an issue, but it was. And I was completely humiliated. By the time a meeting was over, I had already forgotten everything. I was completely unable to stay focused long enough to take notes during meetings, so I just sat there like an idiot, confused and flustered. I was clueless and couldn't absorb any of the information. It was as if I was sitting in the middle of a crowded amusement park wearing ear plugs, frantically trying to process what someone was saying to me. It all sounded like that telephone voice from Charlie Brown.

After the accident, I couldn't do much of anything and I became a hermit. My girlfriend Christina, who was also my neighbor, brought me over a bunch of awesome novels. Unfortunately, I found that I would forget what I had just read, so I constantly had to go back and reread the previous paragraph. Finishing a chapter was impossible, never mind an entire book. I became so frustrated that reading was no longer enjoyable and I even cancelled my book club membership. Reading a 500-page novel used to take me a matter of days, and now I had zero ability to concentrate; I constantly lost focus.

I was also told that I kept repeating myself, but I had no memory of it and would ask people the same question over and over. Mom understood and played along, but it was frustrating for everyone else and embarrassing to me. I thought I had lost my mind in the accident, until I was shown the lengthy reports from Dr. P, a neuropsychologist and cognitive neuroscience specialist I had been sent to in 1998. I had completely forgotten about this specialist, but here were the answers in black and white.

The details of the days I spent with Dr. P came flooding back. After three days of multiple EEGs, EKGs, and other tests with wires and brain caps attached to my skull, he was finally able to explain what was happening with my brain. Due to significant impact to the skull when my head hit the roof of the car, along with the violent force of my head being thrown back, which caused whiplash and the trauma to the brain, it was anticipated that I would always suffer from short- and long-term memory loss, as well as complete lack of focus and concentration.

Any distraction whatsoever would disturb my ability to focus. Minor everyday things, like a gust of wind, someone coughing or sneezing, or a door clicking shut would completely interfere with my train of thought, as well as my ability to remember that thought after the distraction. You can't imagine how frustrating, confusing and incapacitating this was. If something distracted me on the way to the bathroom, I would actually forget the urge to urinate and return to doing what I was doing. The urge would return a few moments later and I would repeat the process until I finally succeeded in relieving myself. I can just imagine what I looked like.

Since I told Dr. P I wanted to return to school someday, he included in his lengthy report a recommendation letter to provide preferential settings, such as isolated and quiet areas for assignments, tests and exams, in addition to allowing a recording device for all classes. These things would be required for learning in my case. The second recommendation was for my mom and I to educate ourselves on the subjects of epilepsy and panic attacks, since there were epileptic and anxiety indications in the readings of my brain activity. He was doubtful that any of my pre-accident memories would return. I was relieved by his revelations, but I must admit, I was also unnerved.

At least I knew I wasn't going crazy; not really anyway. This also explained why I couldn't handle those meetings at the printing company and had struggled so much since the accident with mental processes. I wasn't even able to pass a simple aptitude test. I wish I would have remembered Dr. P's findings prior to accepting the position; I could have saved myself a lot of humiliation. There were so many medical reports that I just couldn't keep up, and with the damage to the brain, this one had eluded me.

I never really accepted the seriousness of these kinds of issues, nor the fact that I wasn't as mentally capable as I used to be. Whether

I just ignored the reports, or had completely forgotten about them, the result was the same, and I had completely humiliated myself again. My confidence was shattered upon hearing the news that I was fired. The words still reverberate in my head. I was so afraid of trying again, but I was certainly not ready to throw in the towel. There had to be something I could do successfully with my life, even taking into consideration the mental and physical limitations. Everyone has a reason for being here, a purpose, don't they? What was mine?

I had to be realistic and accept that I was a "person with disabilities" or history would keep repeating itself. I tried to be honest with myself and accept that I would never be able to do what I used to do so easily. I was a completely different person with different abilities, whether I wanted to be or not. I still so desired to be the pre-accident Marie with all her skills, abilities and talents, but I knew that I no longer had any of these things, and that I had completely taken them for granted. One thing had not changed, and that was my overwhelming need to achieve. I no longer cared about what I succeeded at or accomplished, nor did I have the freedom to, but I desperately needed to accomplish something so I could feel like a somebody again.

This inner voice, it just kept piercing through…

"Marie, you've expressed every self-deprecating judgment possible, yet you are hurt that it's being reflected back to you by others. Your shame, guilt and self-loathing are palpable, and this changes who you are. You are quiet around certain people, ashamed and isolating yourself even more. You are hiding from your loved ones and from the world in shame. What if you absolutely did not care one iota about the opinions, beliefs and judgments of others? What if you absolutely did not care one iota about your own opinions, beliefs and judgments? Can you sense the freedom in this? Being a somebody is what you're desperately seeking, but the seeking itself is keeping you from discovering that you already are everything you could ever dream of… and more.

Do you even realize what you're saying? You are actually aware of your thoughts! If you can perceive your thoughts then you are not your thoughts, are you? Take a step back and just notice the words popping up—without bias, opinion or judgment. Remain neutral; be the witness instead of the participant. It's just a tape continuously playing in your head on an endless loop. Take note of this.

Take a couple of deep breaths, remember that you exist, and that you are not the thoughts. Don't make them personal, because they aren't. And you certainly don't have to believe them. Discover the power of focusing on your breath in meditation, and don't worry if the thoughts don't stop. Just return to the breath as soon as you notice you're back in thought. This is meditation. As you practice daily, you'll notice the gaps becoming longer and longer; the thoughts becoming fewer and farther between.

Are you noticing the glimpses of light along the way? Are you acknowledging the miracles occurring in your life? Be grateful for what you have, instead of being sad about what you don't have. You will have much more to be grateful for—I promise! And this journey will be much easier.

Use your emotions as a "navigation system." They are always accurate. If something feels bad then it's not true; you will fully understand this one day.

There is only abundance. Know that there is no universal law of lack, that lack does not exist. You are abundance itself.

Feel my guidance, know that I am here always and that I love you beyond words. I know you can hear me because you haven't given up. You are still here.

Can you see the signposts that are everywhere? They are highlighted and exaggerated by your emotions, so they should be obvious. Dr. B doesn't make anything wrong. He is supporting you totally without judgment and has complete faith in you. You literally light up in his presence by the beautiful reflection of who you are, and you remember the truth of what you've always been and always will be. Yes, this is also a reflection, and if you could feel the connection itself to the one who inspires you, you would know that this is what you truly are. What you see in others is already in you, otherwise you wouldn't see it; it would be completely oblivious to you. You cannot see in another what is not in you—it's that simple.

Be aware of the signposts, they are everywhere. I know this is your journey and that you can't screw it up, no matter what you do. I'll be here loving you always."

CHAPTER FOUR
Another Graphic Failure

Taking absolutely everything into consideration, especially my successes and failures over the last few years, as well as their contributing factors, I was determined to find a career I could manage. I chose graphic design, as this type of work possessed most of the necessary positive factors I needed in order to be successful. I was lacking in education, but I found a three-month course at a local college that was perfect.

It was a fast-track program and the classes were much smaller than in a regular school setting. This would help tremendously with my concentration, memory and focus, since fewer people in the class would decrease the distractions. To have the ability to sit for extended periods of time I could brace my neck, pad my hip, use a special cushion, and lie down on breaks and over the lunch hour. If all else failed, I could speak with Dr. B about temporarily increasing my dose, since it was only for a three-month period. I was so excited! I really thought I had come up with a realistic and achievable goal. I had even settled part of my claim recently and was able to pay the course fee and the costs for books and supplies.

Within the first week of starting the course I already had problems. There were lots of books and supplies required for each class, notwithstanding the medical aids I needed, so I rented a locker right beside the classroom. The issues with focus and concentration weren't so easily resolved.

The class was indeed very small, but there were still plenty of distractions. I was completely unable to absorb or retain information. I must have been asking the same question repeatedly throughout the day, because the teacher sternly announced that she was not going to keep repeating herself or re-explaining assignments. She added that there was a ton of information to pass on with only three months to do it, and that she was not going to hold back the entire class due to the lack of attention by one student.

I wanted to crawl under my chair and never come out. I was completely humiliated and must have turned five shades of red. This was such foreign territory for me, since I had always excelled in school, from elementary to college, and had dearly loved every one of my teachers. This feeling of inadequacy and shame was becoming way too familiar and I hated it.

I borrowed some money from my godmother and purchased a Mac G4 computer loaded with all the necessary programs. I completed all the assignments at home, at my own pace and on my own time, meeting the special requirements in Dr. P's report. It wasn't enough. I needed instruction, explanation and guidance to actually do the assignments, and although I had hired a tutor, she didn't make house calls. I was blowing it and I had no choice but to come clean.

I was brutally honest with my teacher, as well as the program coordinator. To my complete relief, they were not only empathetic and understanding, but willing to help. They now understood why I kept walking out of classes or was unable to attend at all, and that I was not being rude by repeatedly asking the same questions. The teacher was extremely apologetic for the scene in the classroom. She had become annoyed and irritated because she just could not understand why an adult would invest so much money, time and effort to get into a course, and then not bother showing up or paying attention when she did attend. Once they knew the whole story, I could see the confusion on their faces as to why I would choose to take on such a course. I was wondering the same thing myself.

We collaborated and decided to cut some of my classes, leaving me with fewer subjects to focus on, as well as a day in between to catch up and recover at home. In spite of our combined efforts and all the steps we had taken, it wasn't long before we realized that it just wasn't possible. My pain and mental issues would not allow it, and we all knew it was over.

I kept postponing the inevitable, even though I wasn't learning anything. I just didn't want to give up—until it was too late. I had forced myself to endure another endless day of sitting, until the pain became so excruciating that I began to vomit. As usual, admitting defeat was difficult for me, and this time it was even worse. This was the end of the road for me; my very last hope at a dignified future.

In our last group meeting, we tearfully said our goodbyes and shared best wishes. They offered me a place in the Fall semester at no additional cost if my health improved, and even went as far as saying they knew I would graduate with honors and this would all be a distant memory. It was a beautiful story and I appreciated their thoughtful gestures, although I knew it was a fairy tale. In complete denial, I had talked myself into taking the course, and once again, I had humiliated myself. And I had paid $15,000 to do it. Why did I keep doing this to myself? Because I had to be something, *anything*, to have value.

I was no longer the girl I once knew and was proud to be—the girl who was smart, witty, outgoing, and who always excelled at everything she did. The girl who loved a challenge because she had the confidence to get through anything, no matter what. The girl who was always happy with a big smile on her face and loved meeting new people. The girl who loved every second of life and lived it to the fullest. The daredevil and nature lover who could speak endlessly about the colors surrounding the trees and the positive energies that nature had to offer. The one who always raved about the importance of self-love, making yourself happy and never placing that responsibility onto another. The girl who was healthy and fit, who took extremely good care of herself and thoroughly enjoyed having passionate sex. The one who was always willing to try anything—twice. The girl who was in love with love and was optimistic to a fault. The one who saw the world and all of its people through rose-colored glasses. The girl who could have babies, walk unassisted and take care of herself. The one who knew she was limitless and that anything was possible. The one who believed in the power of self-healing. The one who had so much to offer for the betterment of the world. The girl whose faith was untouchable. The girl who wanted to live.

What had I become? Who was I now? I had zero ability to achieve any of my goals, and I came to the inevitable conclusion that I was nothing; a total and complete failure, falling deeper into depression. Dr. L remained as vigilant as ever, spending many sleepless nights and weekends researching possible strategies to improve my quality of life. I was a perfect and viable candidate for lifelong chronic pain management with narcotics, but was I really going to have to live like this for the rest of my life? Was this the best it was going to get?

I was referred to yet another specialist, an orthopedic surgeon, to discuss fusion of the spine. A minimum of eight vertebras had to be fused, completely immobilizing the upper section of my spine. There was less than a fifty percent chance it would have any effect on the pain, and there was also the risk of paralysis. I was a little put off and dismayed when this orthopedic surgeon told Vincenzo that the two of them could party for a month on the drugs I was taking in a day. They both laughed hysterically. Here I was facing a huge decision with the risk of paralysis, and they were joking around. I eventually decided against the surgery.

Diary Entry, April 2002

At all costs, I must avoid allowing myself to become attached to any more hopeless expectations—my life depends on it. There are no medical solutions or miraculous cures for any of my injuries, and I must face this. I can't fathom being any lower than I am today, but I've believed that before, and here I am.

I no longer have the luxury of self-denial, as this physical torture and depression are continuously worsening. Avoiding any undue stress or disappointment must be my first priority, if there is any chance of making it through this. I must shelter myself from shame and all other situations with possible detrimental effects and feelings. I must isolate myself from everyone in order to battle the frequent episodes of excruciating symptoms and the possible outcomes resulting from chronic pain, in order to lessen the severity of this depression. Or I will kill myself.

After six years of trial and error, I have learned to read my body well; I know what I need to do. At the slightest onset of a migraine, I must immediately take the steps necessary to prevent falling any further down than I already am. I must stay in this apartment to accomplish this and not chance being anywhere other than here.

Most importantly, any and all pain medication must be taken at the very first hint of these symptoms, otherwise the desired effect is no longer possible. For some reason unknown to me, if the pain has the opportunity to become more severe, no pain medication or any amount thereof has any effect whatsoever. This has been my experience for over six years, yet I still resist taking the pain medication. I must be fucked right up to knowingly continue to torture myself like this. What is this resistance to pain medication and the belief that I can fight through this on my own? Why the fuck do I keep doing this to myself?

I was allowing the associated stigma, as well as other peoples' opinions, to dictate how I felt about taking narcotics. This was creating much suffering for myself. There is no way addiction is possible when using narcotics in the treatment of pain. No way. The medication is serving its function by blocking pain signals in the brain, and therefore there is never a high. I have been on massive doses of narcotics, yet I have never experienced even the slightest buzz.

I assume that when there is no purpose for the medication (absence of pain), then a high is reached. But why on earth would anyone consume these medications if they weren't necessary?

High or not, the side effects are not pleasant. I fully understand the long-term effects of taking narcotics, as Dr. B has been very thorough and forthcoming. However, "long-term" isn't even possible without getting through today. How am I supposed to think ahead ten or fifteen years into my future when I feel like I don't even have a future due to the excruciating pain? And how could anyone believe that any person would grow up wishing to have to rely on drugs to have any quality of life whatsoever? Right, this had been my dream, my ultimate dream...

I'm sure there are people who abuse these medications, but why are chronic pain patients punished and judged because of it? Doesn't this clearly indicate that there is an emotional void to be filled, and that it will never be found unless one goes within to discover what the void is? I am certainly not taking narcotics to fill an emotional void, and I have never abused them. Yet the judgment remains. This must stop. If I can't change the judgments of others, I can at least stop judging myself for my pain management protocol.

The insurance claim and the loss of income replacement benefits due to the two assessments confuse me the most. Do insurance companies truly believe that one would willingly put themselves through all this for some chump change? The treatment I received from the insurer is nothing less than thoughtless, brutal and unnecessary. No person would go through these humiliating assessments, put up with such horrific treatment from the insurer, and completely put their life on hold, cutting off their sense of purpose by watching their dreams pass by, unless there was no other choice.

The insurance industry's profit margin would only increase by being encouraging and supportive towards someone's rehabilitation, without judgment and shame. A return to pre-accident duties would result much more quickly, greatly benefitting both parties. The pressure, shame and stress associated with having to rely on external funding, notwithstanding the constant need to prove that you're not a fraud, would be alleviated and a return to health would be imminent.

When the neck, shoulder and upper back muscles seize, all steps are null and void. Complete immobilization is the result, with excruciating pain throughout my entire body. The smallest most insignificant movement or reflex causes atrocious pain referral down my back, under my shoulder blades, through my chest muscles, down my arms and into my fingers. It continues up the back of my head, through the skull, and into the brain and eyes. Even shivering from being cold, or looking to the side sends me into a hysterical frenzy, which is usually followed by a panic attack and/or a seizure.

If this condition coincides with a migraine (which it almost always does), I do not move from my sleeping position, regardless of how long it endures, since I am completely immobilized. I'm constantly urinating all over myself, which is beyond humiliating. Vincenzo has purchased all kinds of pee pads, but it goes right through to the couch, saturating everything. The smell is a constant reminder of how disgusting I am. He wants me to wear diapers but I will not. Ever.

I lay in complete darkness and silence with ice packs from the top of my head to the bottom of my back. Any form of light or sound triggers horrible and sometimes bizarre pain and symptoms, such as throbbing and pounding inside my head and in my muscles, and a totally weird and annoying buzzing or ringing in my ears. It feels like there are a million little ice picks stabbing my brain, my eyes and my ears. It is such a long, painful endeavor to change out the ice packs, for both me and Vincenzo. I'm sure he finds the smell of me very attractive.

I still haven't discovered anything to alleviate any of these symptoms, and since I've refused fusion, with its slight chance of a reduction in my pain, I guess I never will. Quality of life must be first and foremost. I must drop all judgments and beliefs regarding narcotics. I know myself better than anyone, and I am not an addict. Nor could I ever be. I don't even drink alcohol; I never have. I can't even stand the smell of it. I must stop caring about the opinions of others and start listening to myself.

The pain in my hip just keeps worsening, and sitting erect has become impossible. My right leg is seized 100 percent of the time and it feels as if my knee cap is going to pop off at any moment. The pain refers down the shin and into my foot. I'm not sure what is happening, but I still can't bear much weight on that side, and I have fallen on numerous occasions. I just don't feel the leg anymore, and before I know it, I'm on the floor. I must start using the walker at all times, but I hate that stupid thing. I guess it's better than constantly falling to the floor, injuring my neck even more than it already is. Maybe I could use the braces again?

I've been poked, cut, prodded and invaded more times than I can compute. I lost count of the needles many years ago, but I'm sure we must easily be into the thousands. Mom comes over weekly to empty me, since I have lost all ability to have a bowel movement on my own. I don't even remember what the urge feels like. I am too embarrassed to have the nurse come to the house to do it, since then Vincenzo would know. So Mom gently does her thing while making the most ludicrous jokes. Her jokes make it easier, and she even makes me giggle at times. She actually says that I must think my asshole is prettier than hers, since I'm so anal about it. No pun intended.

I have been unable to eat solid foods for as long as I can remember. Even the smell of food coming from the kitchen makes me nauseous. I wonder what it would feel like to go out and enjoy a nice dinner with my husband, or even to have the ability to sit at the kitchen table. I find myself constantly daydreaming of beautifully arranged dishes, with salad and an assortment of vegetables that I used to so thoroughly enjoy—and completely took for granted. The privilege of raising a fork to my mouth, tasting and savoring the favors, has long eluded me. I find myself curiously watching Vincenzo or the people on television mindlessly gulping their food down, having absolutely no clue how blessed they are. They will never realize this unless that ability is taken away, as mine has been.

It is the same with all of the abilities I've lost, I guess. It is morbidly fascinating to remember all the things I used to mindlessly do, like walking without a second thought—or even a shred of gratitude. How endlessly grateful I would be to have any of these abilities now; I would never take any of them for granted again. I would savor every single moment.

In spite of all these experiments, precautions, sacrifices and efforts, most days include several violent episodes of vomiting, and the movement itself makes me scream in horror. It hurts so bad that if there was a gun in my vicinity, I would have used it long ago. These "pain days" usually last two to three days, and my mouth develops really gross and painful sores from the acid in the vomit. My teeth are rotting away.

At this point, I don't even have the will to take any of these necessary steps because deep down inside, I feel I deserve everything I get, including the physical agony. There are many reasons for this complete misery, including constantly peeing all over myself, the vomit, the rotting teeth, the seized upper body, the complete lack of ability to take a shit on my own or even clean myself up, the fact that I can't even sit at a table or eat solid food like a normal person. I can see the way Vincenzo looks at me, and I can't blame him whatsoever. I'm treated like a loser junkie with every visit to the hospital or the pharmacy, and I know my family feels the same. I am a disgusting worthless human being. Who the fuck could live like this?

Surrounding and contouring my entire being is an extra layer of "skin" a few inches from mine, which acts as an invisible barrier to everyone. It is filled with a dark fog of gloom, pain and despair. My loved ones are all around me, trying so hard to reach me, and they can't see why I'm not reaching back. They have become frustrated, sad and angry, for they do not understand. Nor could they.

I feel helpless, alone and unloved, yet I can't get to this outer layer of "skin." I'm stuck frozen in this dark, lonely and unbreakable bubble with a growing sense of being forlorn and desperate. In everyone around me, I see the pain and torment in their souls, but I can't escape. I can't even move. I must sit by watching as my loved ones suffer, and I can't even look away. I'm stuck, and I can't make myself move to pierce the bubble and break free.

There is no way I'm allowing anyone else to see me like this. Deep down inside I know they don't even want to, anyway. I will stay in my bubble and keep them far away, so they won't have to witness any of this anymore.

The depression keeps worsening and I am losing control. We've tried different combinations of antidepressants and countless other cocktails, but the thoughts of suicide are unrelenting. My marriage is falling apart. We are not even 18 months in and my home life is intolerable. Vincenzo calls me his "roommate" since we never share a bed. I can only sleep in a very specific seated position on the couch, with pillows on each side of my head for support, with my back at a 45-degree angle and my feet on a foot stool. Any variation thereof results in unbearable pain the following morning, including my upper back and neck totally seizing-up, which is usually followed by a trip to the hospital. My usual morning routine is severe enough; I literally have to wait until my medication takes effect before attempting any movement at all. Just putting the pills in my mouth and lifting the water bottle is almost too much to bear, causing tears to stream down my face.

I've had to cancel plans so often that I refuse to make any and I no longer answer the phone or talk to anyone. I live in complete darkness. Mom and Vincenzo know not to even go near the blinds, let alone open them. I am falling further and further into the abyss, and because of feelings of unworthiness and shame due to not being able to accomplish anything, I feel like I'm letting everyone down.

I'm hoping my family knows they haven't done anything wrong; that I am pushing them away because I am losing myself. The constant apologies for not being able to go anywhere, be with them or do anything... I just couldn't do it anymore. I had to let them go, and it is ripping out my heart because they eventually gave up on trying to reach me. If I had no legs or arms, if my injuries were visible, they might be able to understand, but they don't. How could they since I don't even understand?

Mom comes over every Friday evening while Vincenzo is at hockey, and all I can see in her eyes is distress. I can see what this is doing to her, and it is literally killing me. I am causing everyone pain, suffering and worry. *(End of diary entry.)*

I wanted to have children, and so did Vincenzo, but I must have subconsciously known that I couldn't, since I kept procrastinating talking about the subject or speaking with Dr. L until my husband put his foot down and demanded answers. Dr. L shook his head from side to side as he looked down at his papers. He whispered the words, "There's no way this is possible. I'm sorry." Not only was I physically incapable of carrying a child, but all of the medications I had to take could seriously harm an unborn child. There was absolutely no possible way.

I must admit that I was relieved when I heard the words, but I was also consumed with guilt. I wanted children so badly, but I knew I couldn't be a mom, and certainly not the kind of mom I had. I was completely unable to look outside of my own pain and misery as I was completely engrossed by agony and depression. How was I going to care for a child when I couldn't even care for myself?

I didn't spend time with my nieces and nephews anymore because I wanted to spare them the disappointment and hurt feelings. I had tried to spend time with them, but I couldn't stick to my commitments. I would tell them I was coming to see them on the weekend, then the pain and depression would take over. I was constantly letting them down. My brother and his wife asked me to be more consistent, but it was impossible, so I stayed away all together. Besides, I wasn't exactly a good role model or setting a good example, regardless of the reasons. I would go a month or sometimes more without washing myself or brushing my teeth. I certainly didn't want anyone to see me like that.

Yes, I was causing everyone I loved pain, suffering and disappointment. One night, I made the decision to kill myself and nothing was going to stop me. I just had to wait for the right time. A time alone when I wouldn't be interrupted.

Vincenzo and I had a long conversation the next day and I was excruciatingly honest, admitting my deepest, darkest secrets. I was so frightened. I brought up the baby subject and he cut me off, telling me that this would all be over soon and that we would be able to start a family. I repeatedly tried to explain the truth to him, but he would not hear me. Whether he just didn't understand, or was choosing not to, I didn't know.

I realized that he was still waiting for the girl he fell in love with to come back—the fitness instructor and Sunshine Girl he met all those years ago. He was holding on for dear life, hoping, wishing and waiting for her. I knew in that moment that I was waiting for her too, and had been for a very long time. But she died the day of the accident, and although I went to extremes attempting to become her again, she wasn't ever coming back.

Vincenzo certainly wasn't willing to trade her for me—and neither was I. And that made my decision much easier. Even that stupid fucking voice couldn't stop me. It was full of shit because there was certainly no hope in hell for me!

"I'm here and I'll never leave you. You are never alone. You are loved and you are love. I'm right here; why can't you feel me? I wish I could lift you out of that bathtub, hold you and carry you the rest of the way, but I know that this is your journey, that you're not ready yet, and that everything is for your highest good. You don't know it now, but someday you'll look back on all of this and see that everything was a gift. You will even express that you would do it all over again. I know you are safe and always have been."

CHAPTER FIVE
The Deep Hell of Depression

I poured myself a bath, placed my bottle of OxyContin on the rim, removed my neck and lower back braces, and carefully climbed in, slowly lowering myself into the warm soothing water. My dead body certainly wouldn't be disgustingly dirty when I was found, and no one would have to clean up afterwards. As I sat there completely detached, I imagined the wonderful lives my loved ones could finally have once I was gone. It made me smile. I thought of my beautiful dogs, Judge and Titus, and knew they would miss me terribly. But somehow I believed that they'd be better off without me as well. I took the pills in a robotic manner, one by one, until I lost count. I slowly drifted off. I would soon be free, and so would everyone I loved.

I awoke with what felt like a sledge hammer to the chest. I was cold, confused and covered in my own vomit. Where was I? I didn't recognize anything around me; everything was distorted and out of focus. I was naked and in ice cold water, but why? Slowly the realization of what I had done came flooding back... and I couldn't believe I had failed yet again.

I began to sob so uncontrollably that my body was violently shuddering, causing the bath water to seep over the edges. I was shivering intensely and I could hear my teeth chattering. My throat was burning and felt like it was on fire from vomiting all the drugs I had taken. I was completely unable to lift my lifeless body for what seemed like hours, as I continued to weep into the mat I had grabbed off the floor. There was no way I was going to call out to Vincenzo for help or let anyone see me like this. Why was I still here? God, why wouldn't you take me? Is this what you call a fucking life? I just can't take another moment of this painful, excruciating existence. Haven't I been through enough?

My legs were shaking so badly from weakness that they wouldn't carry me, but after several attempts I managed to lift myself out using my arms. Like a dead fish landing in the bottom of a boat, my body dropped with a thud onto the bathroom floor. I grabbed all the towels that were within reach, wrapping them around my cold body. I was so numb.

The thought of failing at even this haunted me to the core of my being, resulting in shame unlike anything I had ever felt before. With my head buried in the towels, I continued to weep. How would I face anyone? Everyone would know. I had to hide this somehow, but what if it had done even more damage to my body? I had to at least tell Dr. L.

After what seemed like forever, I pulled myself up off the floor using the door knob. The moment I stepped out, I was face-to-face with my husband. The smell of vomit alone must have given me away, but also the almost empty bottle of OxyContin still sitting on the edge of the bathtub and the yellowish green vomit floating in the water. I turned away in shame. I will never repeat his cruel words, but those words, along with the look of complete disgust on his face, drove a dagger through my heart that would take years to remove.

Still unable to hold my weight, I crawled to the couch and collapsed from sheer exhaustion. My eyes were so swollen that I couldn't keep them open.

I woke up to the feeling of pressure against my body, the warmth of breath on my face and the unmistakable sensation of doggy kisses. I opened my eyes to see Judge, my king Doberman, licking my tears away. Oh, how I loved this creature with all my heart! More tears sprang to my eyes from a wave of sheer gratitude for his presence. He still loved me—-unconditionally. I didn't deserve him. I had just tried to abandon him. I wept as I held him tightly, begging for forgiveness. He had never left my side for anything or anyone since the day I brought him home, just shortly after the accident. He had given me such purpose, such joy and such unconditional love. He was the only reason I had made it through the first few months of the accident. And here he still was, without judgment, unconditionally loving me. I held on even tighter. How I wished I could see myself through his soulful eyes.

Realizing I was still covered in my own vomit and layers of damp towels, and desperately needing to go the bathroom, I reached for my medication, knowing I couldn't even think of moving until its effects had kicked in. Judge remained by my side, as he always did, and continued to keep my body, as well as my heart, warm. After a few minutes, I could feel some relief from the agonizing pain, but soon I realized I had peed myself again. I was able to slowly make my way to the bathroom to clean myself off a bit, but the sight of my refection in the mirror made me gasp in horror.

What had I become? As I studied every inch of my face, there was absolutely no resemblance to the girl in all those pictures hanging on the walls of our apartment. Who was this person with matted hair, red swollen eyes, vomit-stained skin, soaked pajama bottoms, and a gaunt, haunted look staring back at me? I turned away in shame. Again, I saw Judge looking up at me with the most adoring eyes. I couldn't understand what he was seeing, but I felt the love nonetheless. How different things would have been had it not been for this once-in-a-lifetime boy.

Mom and I went to Dr. L's office. An assortment of new medications had been added to my already overloaded system. I discovered that Mom had secretly contacted Dr L earlier that week, due to my dreadful appearance. She was distraught with worry. Upon entering his office, I could see the frantic look in his eyes as he carefully inspected me from head to toe. I was twenty pounds lighter than the last time he saw me, and in the exact same dirty, urine-soaked pajamas, which were now hanging off of me.

It was so hard to admit it to him, but I hadn't bathed or even washed since the suicide attempt five weeks prior. I was disgusting and disgraceful. As I lowered my eyes in shame, he rose from his chair and took me in his arms, not caring for one second about the smell that was emanating from me. I couldn't hold it in for one more second and I broke down, sobbing into his expensive jacket as Mom watched with tears rolling down her face.

All I could mutter through my sobbing gasps was, "Dr. L, I tried to kill myself. I'm so sorry. I'm so sorry, Mom, that I couldn't tell you. Mom, I tried to kill myself. I'm so sorry. I should have come to you, Mom. I should have run to you. I'm so sorry." Mom rushed over and took us both in her arms as my knees buckled beneath me. There I was, surrounded by love in the middle of a doctor's examination room in an empty building, since the office closing hours had long passed. What had I done?

Depression is a dark and lonely place, filled with nothing but hopelessness, shame and helplessness. I felt overwhelmingly detached from the world and everyone in it, including the ones I loved and cherished. I missed them so much it hurt, in a way I couldn't possibly express. I wished I could just move to a tiny little house in the middle of nowhere, miles from any civilization, with no road or telephone access, just a small two-way radio for emergencies, and all of my necessary supplies dropped by helicopter once every couple of months.

Of course my dogs would be with me and totally free. On my imaginary isolated land I'd have the ability to care for them. Walks and leashes wouldn't be necessary; all I would have to do is open the door. I would never come back. The constant burden of causing nothing but grief to the ones I loved the most would be over, and they could finally be free as well. I realized that they would be hurt initially, but eventually this would come to an end and they'd forget about me. They would never again have to be a witness to this pain, this despair, and this meaningless life. Oh, how I dreamed of this! I envisioned every little detail. If I couldn't succeed at killing myself, then this was the next best thing. At least I got to experience it in my dreams.

I had always been taught that anything is possible when you put your mind to it and your heart in it. I should be able to snap myself out of this and make myself better. You can't imagine how disheartening these kinds of sayings are to a person suffering from clinical depression and chronic pain. I had heard so many well-meaning people say such things like, "You're just in a rut." "Just snap out of it." "Just get up, brush yourself off and do it." "Think positive." "Remember that there are a lot of people out there much worse off than you." "Everyone has problems." "Talk yourself out of this slump and make the decision to stop living like this." "Just get dressed, go out for a little while and do something, it will make you feel better." And the worst one of them all, which is something my Mémére used to say all the time, "Un petit coup de coeur," which means "a little bit of heart." Mom would often lovingly say this to me, obviously not knowing it would crush me every single time.

The reason these words are often said by well-meaning people is because depression and chronic pain are tremendously misunderstood unless you've been through it yourself. Being told I had chronic pain, in addition to clinical depression, and that I would suffer from these conditions for the rest of my life felt like an accusation, not a diagnosis. It made me feel like I'd done something wrong, that I deserved to be judged and punished, and that I was too weak to just deal with it.

The feelings of remorse, disgrace, blame, contempt, and complete and utter mortification were like an avalanche that simply grew and grew, leading to more of the same. Most people hide it and isolate themselves—just as I did. Go through each well-meaning saying again, but change the diagnosis to cancer, ALS, MS or any "real" disease. Would any of these mindless comments ever be said to a person dealing with cancer, ALS or MS? I already know your answer. Of course not! These diseases are considered to be serious and dangerous, with horrendous, debilitating symptoms. They are visible, well-known, comprehensible and socially accepted as something horrible that happens to good people. They are also well researched and widely studied, with clearly-defined treatments.

I'll never forget the article I read in MacLean's magazine regarding depression. This quote haunts me: "At least with cancer, you die. With depression, you are buried alive." No truer words! Continued persistent depressive disorder and chronic pain were very real to me, but because of the lack of research and interest, no one knows precisely what causes it. All I knew was that depression is a disorder of the brain, an imbalance in serotonin and other chemicals that produces physical, mental and emotional symptoms. And mine was instigated by chronic pain.

With the help of selective serotonin re-uptake inhibitors (SSRIs) and other anti-depressants, some people recover and show substantial improvement; sometimes within weeks. This recovery is not possible with chronic pain, however. So, unless the physical impairment was rectified, alleviating the pain, there was no cure for my depression.

This was 2002, and the most up-to-date treatment for depression relied on the science and art of administering and combining any of the hundreds of available antidepressants, along with a chaser of tranquilizers, anti-seizure drugs or other medications that might balance or augment their effects. Each and every person diagnosed with depression is completely unique, and therefore must journey through a pharmaceutical odyssey that may never end—and usually doesn't. The recovery prospect for this disease is low. The odds of substantial improvement, enough to live a semi-normal life, are even lower.

I had done endless research on the subject, but unfortunately, since chronic pain was the cause of my depression, my pharmaceutical odyssey consisted only of finding a way to somehow minimize the unbearable, all-consuming symptoms. Only this would lead to giving me the will to live.

Besides all of our failed efforts at finding the magic concoction (if one even existed), the hardest thing to cope with was that my physical impairments, mental instability, emotional anguish and relentless pain were not visible. I was completely engulfed by a dark and morbid hell of misery, and it was invisible to everyone but me.

This hell of misery reached into every cell of my body and weighed me down with a crushing fatigue. I couldn't move. I couldn't think. I couldn't focus long enough to read. I was alone even when surrounded by loved ones.

In this six-year pharmaceutical journey, some medication helped, but didn't last; some didn't help at all. With some, the side effects proved intolerable—I would shake and sweat profusely, yet I was shivering and twitching from being cold; my heart was racing, yet I was tired and completely unable to sleep; I suffered massive weight gain and complete loss of libido; I was mentally and emotionally numb and unresponsive... and so on and so on. This vicious cycle continued until I was taking more than 70 pills a day.

I remember there was one medication that actually had a positive effect. The clouds finally parted and I could feel the sun reviving my body and my soul. After being denied this for countless years , I can't even begin to explain how good it felt. There was actually a real unforced smile on my face and joy in my heart! But as fast as the relief came, it left and I hit rock bottom once again.

Not wanting to ever again cause Mom the agony I had caused the last time I attempted suicide, I fought with every ounce of strength I had left to not swallow every pill I had in the house. Although I had confided in Dr. L the most, no one knew the hold this depression had on me, the extent of the despair I was experiencing, or the persistence of my obsession with suicide. However, the worry in Mom's eyes told me that she knew everything.

Diary Entry, November 2002

I'm alone on the battlefield with these invisible attackers, completely defenseless. There must be something, anything, that can provide even the slightest hint of relief from the intensity of this depression and its overwhelming, debilitating effects. Even if it's an insignificant lift, just sufficient enough to give me an ounce of will, or even a quarter of an ounce. Just enough will to *want*; that is all I'm begging for. The will to want. The will to want to move, to want to wash, to want to talk, to want to leave the four square walls of my living room, my prison cell. The want to care about myself, the want to hope, the want to stop neglecting my mom, my dad, my brothers and their beautiful families, my dogs, myself. The want to live... God, I'm begging.

This depression not only kills my will to live, but completely disconnects my inner resources and strength, which would make it possible to fight it. As I'm sitting in my invincible prison cell at this very moment, I resign myself to the possibility of having chronic pain, facing countless more surgeries/procedures and being treated with massive amounts of narcotics for the rest of my life. However, I cannot resign myself to living with this depression for much longer. I won't. I can't.

There has got to be something that can provide even a small amount of relief... is there? Am I holding onto false hopes again? Is this going to take another six long years to realize as well? Is this the reality of my life forever? The constant dreaded bouts of overwhelming desire to take my own life terrorize me. It's as if I've been removed from the equation, like I've been possessed by some indomitable force. This lack of self-control really frightens me and I'm worried that any day now I won't make it through this. I must tell Mom. I must tell her to remove all the medications from this apartment and lock them away in hers. I must find the courage to tell her the truth before it's too late because I will succeed the next time. I know what I did wrong in my first attempt.

This is going to hurt her so badly again, but I must tell her! How do I look into those unconditionally loving eyes and tell her that I just want to die? After all she's done, all she is...
    (End of diary entry.)
The conversation with Mom took place the day after I wrote this diary entry. I will never forget the look of complete relief on her face or the collapsing of her shoulders, as if exhaling for the first time in months. Although I had not told her any of this,

she knew. She knew everything. The connection between us was unlike any mother-daughter relationship I had ever heard of. Words just weren't necessary; she felt every single thing I did and knew instantly when something was wrong. She was an extremely sound sleeper, nothing would wake her up. We could throw a party in the middle of her bedroom and she would just keep snoring away. Yet one whisper of "Mom" sat her straight up from a deep sleep. I thought all the years of caring for me had given her this superpower ability, but she told me that she had been like this with us since we were kids, and I believe her.

The peace of mind from having no access to the necessary ingredients to kill myself was immense, and I began to relax a little, knowing this was now impossible. Mom picked up my prescriptions at the pharmacy once a month and brought them directly to her apartment. She filled the pill pods, carefully following the instructions on the bottles, and at the end of each day, she brought me one pod.

The familiar voice; it just wouldn't give up…

"Marie, the answers you are seeking are already within you. Stop looking everywhere else and just look within; you've had the light all along. The mind-altering medications, in addition to their side-effects, are preventing you from finding the very thing you are looking for. Seeking the answers anywhere outside of yourself will keep you from finding them. The act of seeking itself will keep you from remembering that you are already perfect and whole.

Love yourself unconditionally, and this means no conditions, including the urine, the vomit and the smell. Love everything, all of it, unconditionally. You are falling deeper and deeper into the pit of darkness because you're not remembering the light that you already are, always have been and always will be. You aren't doing anything wrong, so don't make it so.

This is your journey, and I will love you through it. I promise and I know you can hear me. This will be the greatest blessing of your life one day... and you will get there. You will be overwhelmed by the thought of the miracles you would have missed had you succeeded in taking your own life. This I know. And you will be flabbergasted by the simplicity of the answer you are so desperately seeking.

Remember that you have never experienced anything other than the dance and your reaction to it. Are you going with the flow of the music, effortlessly swaying your body? Or are you fighting against the beat every step of the way? Dance, my beauty. Just let go and dance. Take my hand and follow my lead."

CHAPTER SIX
The Loss

I remember all too well hearing about people wanting to commit suicide and some actually going through with it. I would always think to myself, "Give me a break; suck it up buttercup. How could anyone do such a thing or even think about it? It's absolutely crazy, nobody can be that weak. They must be total whiners just looking for attention. I am way too strong to let anything bum me out that much. And physical pain driving you to kill yourself or stop living life? Unbelievable. I've had lots of pain in my life from competing in gymnastics and training to be a police officer. I've had broken bones, surgeries to remove my tonsils in my teens and so on. I got over it and it wasn't a big deal. These people must be total victims and I certainly can't be around them. What total downers! I'd have to smack them upside the head."

Gosh, what little did I know. My uneducated and completely misinformed assumptions were pathetic. Judgments and assumptions always are, unless the situation is experienced for oneself. And even then, they are filtered through a lens, creating bias. I could never have imagined that this would happen to me, not in a million years. I thought suicide was for weaklings who only thought about themselves. It made me sick that a person could feel so sorry for themselves that they would bring so much pain to their loved ones.

"How could they choose such an easy way out?" was a question I asked myself when I heard of such stories. Could they not see all the real suffering in the world and understand how lucky they are? There are homeless, starving, abused and neglected children, victims of racism, genocide, slavery, rape and murder. Innocent families are assaulted and robbed, helplessly having to watch it all happen. Women are stuck in horribly abusive and torturous relationships with no way out. How shallow can these suicidal people be? Do they not ever think of all these people with real problems? The judgments I so heartlessly made were exactly the same judgments with which I was now forced to cope. How ironic.

A person can never even come close to relating to depression, chronic pain, or any other illness for that matter, unless it's personally experienced. I knew this firsthand, yet sometimes I still perceived myself in the exact same way I used to perceive others suffering from depression, chronic pain, or any of the other "invisible" illnesses. That's what made this so difficult. I would think about all of those who were so much worse off than me, and fall into a pit of self-loathing and disgust. How could I be so shallow and weak?

I would think of Mom's face after my suicide attempt, feel the pain and anguish she was suffering, and I would cry for her. The devastation and agony that ending my own life would cause her would be unspeakable, and she would blame herself for the rest of her life. She is the most beautiful and selfless human being. She has loved me unconditionally and cared for me each and every moment of each and every day for 31 years. There was no way I could cause her such grief. I believed it was an act of love at the time, that I was freeing her from the shackles I had put on her, but after seeing the pain in her eyes upon hearing my confession, I knew nothing could be further from the truth. We needed each other, and even though I was a burden and couldn't care for myself, she was willingly, lovingly helping me every step of the way. Although I could never repay her, I would certainly do my very best to try... someday.

Vincenzo had been miserable for months. His periods of impatience and anger had become much worse since the development of my latest affliction, eczema, brought on by constant stress. My hands looked like two big chunks of raw hamburger covered in lesions, cracks, bubbles, scabs and blood. The skin specialist firmly declared that in no uncertain terms was I ever to have my hands even near water, and I had to sleep wearing surgical gloves coated on the inside with cortisone.

Although this condition was extremely painful, and the itching could drive somebody mad, I think my husband was just overwhelmed and angry that he now had even more responsibility than he did before, since I could no longer do my one little chore—washing the dishes. Any perceived inconvenience, like the dogs needing to go out, Mom calling or stopping in, or seeing me cry, would throw him into such an ugly mood that I distanced myself even further. Between these angry stretches of barking and snapping at me, he would completely ignore me as if I wasn't there.

Our marriage was over. I had long known this, and actually I knew we were doomed from the very beginning. Approximately four months prior to the wedding, I had spoken to him at length about the severity of my condition and my complete inability to care for myself, and told him that this responsibility would fall on his shoulders. I said that he deserved a girl who could love him the way he deserved to be loved; not one who couldn't even find a way to love or accept herself. I was setting him free and encouraging him to walk away, but he adamantly refused and talked me into going through with this charade. We were both in complete denial. There was also something else holding me back, but I wouldn't allow myself to even think about this at the time. I wasn't worthy of the one whom I had never let go of, nor would I ever be.

Vincenzo was a kind, considerate and loving man prior to our marriage, and I should have walked away then. But I wanted children and a family, and I did love him. I was so very confused about our marriage, and I tried to remind myself during his frequent miserable moods of everything he had sacrificed. But it hurt so bad to be treated in such a horrible way. I fell further down every time and truly could not handle this in my condition. He was completely justified in his feelings of frustration, disappointment and anger about our relationship, but I was dying a little more each day. I desperately needed his support and understanding. If he truly loved me, how could he even conceive of causing me more pain and suffering? I knew he could clearly see the effects of his hurtful words and actions on my fragile state of mind and body. I couldn't take it anymore.

Diary Entry, February 2003

All of this stress is sending me right over the edge. Feeling overwhelmed with sorrow and anxiety, and desperately needing to escape, I almost left him the other night. Where the fuck am I supposed to go without a dime to my name? I'm trapped and there's no way Mom can support me again. Is she supposed to get a third job instead of sleeping? Leaving would be the best; I know it. He may not know it now, but he soon will, beyond a shadow of a doubt.

I know for a fact that he hates this life and this so-called "relationship," but if he can't control his moods and stop these angry outbursts immediately I'm going to lose it. I'm already struggling, so what the fuck is he thinking? If I was the old Marie, I would knock him out with a stiff upper-cut followed by a hook. And maybe even a throat punch for good measure. Actually, if I was the old Marie there would be no need to; he wouldn't be like this and we might even have been happy together. I know he won't be able to control his anger because of the pressure constantly weighing on his heart, but does this mean I deserve to be treated like this? But I am the cause of all of this! Even if this was Kevin, my first love, I'm sure he'd be reacting the same way to this pitiful existence. What man wouldn't feel frustrated, discouraged and disgusted with me? I am so confused. How can I give any man the love he so desperately deserves when I can't even love myself? How can I bring happiness into anyone's life when I am lost in a pit of hell filled with sadness and despair?

When I do leave, I will never again be with another man. Ever. I will never again subject myself or anyone else to this existence.

I will be alone for the rest of my life, and I will never allow anyone to get close to me ever again. I will lock that part of my heart up and throw away the key.

As I sit here twirling Kevin's promise ring, which has never left my finger, I know I have the reminder of our love to last me for eternity. I am so relieved that I never threw it away on that awful day at my brother's and his wife's cottage a few weeks prior to my wedding with Vincenzo. Although I had certainly tried. I think of my first love often and hope to God he's loved beyond anything he can fathom, and that all of his dreams have come true. I am so relieved we parted ways before the accident because I know he never would have left, being the type of man he is. It would have crushed me to not be able to give him children and to see him stuck in this kind of relationship. He deserves mad crazy love and ecstatic happiness, and I have nothing to offer. Vincenzo deserves that too, and I hope he someday finds it.

On that fateful day, seven long and agonizing years ago, I truly believed I had survived the accident. But I had not. The Marie I knew died, and the one who is writing these words I don't know or even remotely love. If a video could have been played on that fateful day, showing me my future, the person I would become, the life I would be living and the pain I would cause my loved ones, I would have ended it right there and then. I know of no other who, faced with such a convoluted fate, would choose otherwise. Is it possible that in seven years from now these words will be rewritten? Oh my God, this thought fills me with such dread. Someone please tell me that this won't happen. God, please give me a sign, I'm begging you.

I'm sure there was no video playing in the ambulance, but this memory keeps flashing in my mind of a young man named Dan. In a whisper it seemed, he told me that I was going to be just fine, that I wasn't alone, nor would I ever be, and that God would never abandon me. I studied his face as he carefully ensured my hair wasn't entangled in the straps and buckles of the backboard and neck immobilizer by gently brushing it aside with his large but gentle hands. He was angelic, and his presence brought about instant feelings of calm and awe in me. The love I felt for him, and still do, was from the depths of my soul. But I have no understanding as to why; he was a total stranger. I must find him someday and profusely thank him for being such an angel that day, but to also tell him how wrong he was in his prediction. I must find those ambulance records. *(End of diary entry.)*

I received notification from the insurer that I was being sent to four specialists in Ottawa—an orthopedic surgeon, a pain specialist, a psychiatrist and a neurologist—for an in-depth examination and assessment. I wasn't worried in the least. I had been sent to another specialist in 2001 to determine whether the medications I was taking were necessary and justified, and everything had gone beautifully. The doctor was kind, compassionate and knowledgeable, and he had done a thorough examination. He had obviously read my medical records and reports since he was well-informed as to my injuries, as well as the multitude of diagnoses, and nothing had been rushed or ignored. He paid careful attention to every detail, which was evident in his report to the insurer.

His report basically reiterated what Dr. B had been saying all along—that the medication was necessary and justified for treatment, that nothing was out of order, and that the doses would continuously increase due to tolerance. Little does this doctor know that he literally restored my faith in independent medical examiners and the Hippocratic Oath, since I had been truly disillusioned by the first two nightmares I had experienced with the five-minute doctor and the back institute.

The first appointment came, and although it took everything I had to get off the couch and get myself cleaned, I made it with Vincenzo assisting me. Everything went really well. The doctor was well-informed, kind and compassionate, and took great care of me. The next appointment came soon thereafter, and unfortunately left me in shambles. I will not go into detail as to what happened that day, but I'll just say that my husband was not allowed in the room, and I have never felt so ridiculed and violated in my entire life.

This man was not a human being, he was a monster. and I was left reeling. I confided in Mom, and she was livid. I'm shocked to this day that she didn't go over there and beat the living crap out of him. She was not going to let me go to any future appointments without her.

The third appointment was with the psychiatrist. As the well-dressed man entered the small waiting room and called my name, motioning me to follow him, Mom immediately stood up and grabbed my arm, which totally surprised the doctor. He asked why a woman in her thirties would need her mom to hold her hand, but soon he saw the tears falling down my face and reached out to me with kindness. He gently motioned again and said that I would be just fine.

In his office, with a trembling lip and through the tears , I managed to tell him what had happened at my last appointment. He was stunned and perturbed and wrote everything down. Then he softly assured me that no such thing would take place with him, nor should it have happened in the first place. He was such a special person and wonderful doctor that I wanted him to take me on as a patient. I felt a connection with him and knew that he could help me. Let's just say he wasn't a typical psychiatrist; he was very unique. However, there was a conflict of interest. Since the insurance company had hired him to assess me, I couldn't hire him.

Mom brought me to the last appointment, the neurologist, and everything went well again. He even waved to Mom, inviting her into the examination room. He was knowledgeable, compassionate and a wonderful listener. He also had the kindest eyes, which I will never forget.

My case had long been ignored by the firm I was dealing with, so I had been interacting with the insurance company on my own for a couple of years. However, the new claim representative was such a sweetheart that this wasn't in the least troublesome. I actually enjoyed speaking with him every chance I got. I knew these reports would take a while, since it took multiple banker's boxes to hold my medical files, in addition to the amount of information gathered the day of the examinations and all the specific questions they had to answer in their detailed reports for the insurance company.

These outings and examinations had caused a major increase in my pain symptoms, but that was soon rectified by Dr. B. After an examination and some discussion, the dosage of the OxyContin was increased. As I sat there looking across at my hero, my mentor, and someone I considered a friend, I couldn't help but feel immensely grateful for him. He meant so much more to me than just a doctor, and he would always hold a very special place in my heart for everything he had done for me and for everything he was. I held him in such high esteem, which he deserved in every way, and still does to this day. He gave me the greatest gift one could ever give, and that was belief in myself. He was a gift from God; such a blessing. I can honestly say that without him, I would not be here.

Hobbling through the park on a beautiful sunny day a couple of weeks later, I noticed a golf ball-sized lump on Judge's leg. I thought he must have slammed into a tree chasing squirrels. I called my vet, Helen, when we got home, and took Judge in that very afternoon. She checked out his leg after the sedation took effect. She wasn't really concerned, since cancer mostly attacks the joints, and this lump was in the middle of the leg bone. She decided to take a few x-ray images just to be safe. As I was standing beside the table Judge was laying on, gently stroking him while waiting for the results, I couldn't believe the love I felt for this being. He was the most beautiful dog I had ever seen, and he had loved me through it all, never leaving my side.

My thoughts were interrupted as the door creaked open and I caught the look on the vet tech's face. She told me that Helen wanted to see me in the imaging room where the light board was. A feeling of dread filled me instantly, as I let go of Judge and walked into the room where Helen was waiting. Her sadness was obvious as she pointed to all the holes in Judge's bones. She didn't understand how he could have been chasing squirrels that very morning, or even walking for that matter. She continued by telling me it was cruel to let him go on this way. He was suffering greatly from bone cancer, and had been for a very long time.

I couldn't believe it. I wouldn't believe it. How was I going to live without him? Through almost silent whimpers I said I was bringing him home; that his last day was not going to be spent in a vet's office, and that they could come to the apartment the next day to euthanize him.

Sitting in my spot on the couch with Judge laying in my lap, I held and stroked him all night long, not stopping for even a second. Memories of our last eight years together drifted through my mind like a heartwarming movie, and I was filled with love for this beautiful boy. I wasn't going to let him suffer, but I knew this was the hardest thing I would ever have to do. He lifted his head every so often and lovingly looked at me, holding my gaze for a very long time. I knew what he was waiting to hear, but I didn't know if I could utter the words. Tears rolled down my cheeks. Holding him as gently as I could, I told him that mommy was going to be okay without him, that I loved him more than life itself, and that I would cherish his memory for eternity. I told him I would remember him and all he had done for me, including helping me to walk again. I began sobbing uncontrollably, and once again, he licked away my tears. My Judge. My beautiful Judge. I will love you forever.

Morning came more quickly than I'd hoped, and Helen and Diane were at the apartment ready to do what they came to do. Mom brought Titus, my English Mastiff, over to her place, as I didn't want him to watch what was going to happen to his brother without any understanding as to why. Helen looked up at me with tears in her eyes and asked if I was ready. I nodded my head yes. I couldn't speak. I held my boy tightly, repeatedly telling him how much mommy loved him and that it was time for him to let go. I tried to be strong for him, but the tears just wouldn't stop. I could already feel the emptiness he would leave behind.

He was snoring loudly while his jowls flopped on each exhalation; he was sound asleep and completely unaware. I had been holding him so tightly that I could no longer feel my arms, but I would not let go, even for a second. The needle to stop his heart was next, and it didn't take long for Judge to gently slip away. He was gone. I sobbed uncontrollably as I held him one last time before they took him away. I promised him that I would love his mommy as he had loved her, that I wouldn't hurt her ever again, and that I wouldn't let him down.

The emptiness Judge left was more profound than anything I could have imagined. I could not have prepared myself for this. I spent the next week or so crying myself to sleep every night and waking in tears. At times I could no longer see through the slits of my eyes. Titus stayed close, but obviously he couldn't understand. Or so I thought. Little did I realize that he was grieving too. I invited him up on the couch where Judge used to lay and held him tightly as I cried. All of a sudden, I could feel the warmth of his breath on my face as he was gently licking away my tears. We were grieving together, and he had taken over his brother's job of taking care of mommy.

Shortly thereafter, I left my husband and moved back in with Mom. We soon realized that her apartment was way too small for both of us plus a 262-pound dog. We moved into a townhouse a couple of months later and my divorce soon followed.

The familiar voice was getting louder and I could no longer ignore it…

"Marie! Look at what you've written, Marie. My gosh, read what you've written! The judgments you've assigned to everyone around you are the same judgements you have about yourself, and that are reflected back to you by the outside world. Are these judgments actually being made towards you? This is how you feel about yourself and what you are telling yourself repeatedly throughout the day. Could you be projecting these judgments and assuming that this is how people are seeing you?

For once, be with your brothers and their families and drop any preconceived notions about what they may be thinking about you. Can you not see that you are the one judging them, and that they have absolutely no inkling of what you are going through, since you haven't been honest with them about anything? You are isolating yourself from the people who love you and who would gladly do everything in their power to help you through this. I know they would. And forcing Mom to keep your dark secrets to herself—what do you think that is doing to her relationship with them?

You say you are detached and numb, yet you're putting so much emphasis on the opinions of others, instead of seeing them for what they truly are—pure love. You have pushed them away, not the other way around. You never let them in. Yes, there were some judgments made at the beginning, but why did you care so much, to the point where you completely removed yourself from their lives?

I'm with you and I have your back more than you could ever know. None of these beliefs, opinions and judgments, including your own, have any basis in reality whatsoever, unless you give them that power. And you are. Your current circumstances are based on past thoughts, that's all. Change your thoughts right now. Plant new seeds and you'll soon be rejoicing in the fruits of your labor with a bounty of the most beautiful flowers. Keep what you want the most in mind, what excites you, and don't let the ego deceive you when doubts, challenges and obstacles pop up. Stay the course.

Any way you choose to continue this journey can't be wrong. Know this. I'm just hoping that you'll soon realize the absolutely blissful path you can hop on at any time, and that your circumstances are completely irrelevant and not stopping you from taking this leap.

Dan is an angel, Marie! He's your Guardian Angel. He was in that car, he was in the ambulance , he was everywhere protecting you on that cold January day in 1996. He has never left you, nor could he ever. He can see much more than you can, and he offered you the complete truth. You'll know this one day when you discover that there was no Dan, or anyone fitting that description , in any of the ambulance reports. Dan is an angel; he never was a human.

(**Note:** When I called the hospital, they stated there never was a man named "Dan" in the ambulance, nor anyone fitting his description. There was an older gentleman in the ambulance and a female medic driving. I saw "Dan" as a 20-year-old.)

This older man didn't gently untangle your hair the way Dan did. You were so blessed to be protected and to be able to *see* the angel taking care of you, Marie.

Every time you don't know how much you have left in the tank, this long-haired kid named Roger Federer will inspire you. You sobbed as you watched him fall to the grass upon winning his first Wimbledon. You wept as you saw him lift the trophy, screaming that if he could achieve what he was achieving then you could too. Yes Marie! Yes. He dances with the ball, gracefully moving on his side of the net, never once fighting his opponent. He plays his game, always. You watch and are mesmerized as he orchestrates such a breathtaking dance, which is inspiring you to dance your own dance. Feel the recognition in Roger, what inspires you about him, and remember what you're made of. Play your game, Marie. And dance your dance.

Dr. B, your hero, your mentor, and the one who is always there for you, doesn't make anything wrong. He allows you to be vulnerable without fear of judgment, making your quality of life his number one priority. He's fearless, compassionate and powerful. He sees what is in you, and helps you to recognize it as well. Feel the connection itself to what inspires you in Dr. B, and know that this is also in you... and always has been. He constantly reminds you of who you really are.

The way Judge made you feel—that is who you truly are. Judge filled you with so much love that you thought your heart would burst every time you looked at him—that is who you truly are. The reflection in his eyes is your true reflection. Some part of you must know this, or you wouldn't have made such a heartfelt promise to him. The love you shared with him can never die and will live on for eternity.

You read "The Secret[1]." You watched the movie and you know all about the Law of Attraction. You even removed the piece of paper with the image of the genie from the DVD case, and wrote down all of your biggest hopes and dreams—with Kevin at the very top of the list.

I know you've forgotten this, but someday you will find this long-lost piece of paper and you won't believe your eyes. Every single dream listed will have come true, and you will be filled with so much love, gratitude and awe, that you will cry with glee. And yes, so will Kevin.

CHAPTER SEVEN

Exciting Inner Discoveries

The next few months were busier than usual as Mom, Titus and I were settling into our townhouse and had moved away from Vincenzo's building. Something had dramatically changed. After a wonderful discussion with Dr. B and his words of encouragement on the subject, I began practicing daily meditation. What did I have to lose? I couldn't find much information regarding meditation at the time, but I knew that I had to relax my body and focus on the breath.

The crippling panic attacks (to the point of losing consciousness) were long gone and I had no idea why. I had a renewed sense of hope as the days went on. The physical pain wasn't so debilitating either, which allowed me to lower the narcotic dosage.

I'll never forget the day I became fully aware of the tape that was playing in my head on a continuous loop, and the words it was endlessly repeating. I was so completely shocked that I'm sure my jaw must have dropped open. I opened my eyes, grabbed a pen and began recording everything I had witnessed. As I read back what I had written, I knew exactly why I had been in such pain and distress, filled with crippling anxiety and suicidal thoughts for so many years. How could I not be?

- I am worthless
- I am a waste of skin

- I can't do anything for myself
- I am useless
- I am just a burden
- I am in so much pain
- This pain is intolerable
- I should be stronger than this
- I am so depressed
- I am so tired
- I am so disgusting
- I am so fat
- I am so ugly
- I am useless
- I am unlovable
- I am in so much pain
- My body hurts so bad
- My life sucks
- I will never get better
- I have to take drugs just to move
- I have no life
- I just want to die

I could continue, but I'm sure you get the point. These thoughts were playing in an endless loop in my head, perpetuating every single experience I was having. I was completely unaware that I was saying this to myself, but this was exactly what was happening in my life and how I was feeling. How could it be any different?

I was fully educated in stress factors, fight or fight response, cortisol and other stress hormones, as well as the fact that, to the body, there is no differentiation between a thought and an actual occurrence. My body wasn't under constant attack from chronic pain and depression, it was under constant attack from my thoughts—and it was responding accordingly. I was literally stunned by the venomous, hateful things I was saying about myself, my body and my life. My sole focus became paying attention to the deluge of thoughts while remaining completely neutral, taking away all their power. This became a way of life.

I meditated every single day without fail. I started walking Titus every day, going to the dog park with Mom, talking with people again and actually enjoying myself. The smiles and laughter weren't forced anymore and the weight I had gained melted off. I didn't yet fully understand why everything had changed so dramatically, but I was ecstatic to say the least.

As I lifted the handful of pills to my mouth, a thought popped into my head, and I just couldn't ignore it, as I had become an expert in being aware of my thoughts: "Don't take them; you don't need them." Just the thought of not taking these medications excited me more than I can express, and I made the sudden and drastic decision to stop taking all the anti-depressants, anti-psychotics, anti-anxiety and anti-seizure medications I had been on for years.

A sense of joy swept over me as I put the pills back in the bottle and removed the rest of them from the pill pods. I was elated! I rejoiced in my decision as I glimpsed a sense of freedom I hadn't felt in many years. I couldn't wait to tell Dr. L that he no longer needed to prescribe all these medications because I didn't need them anymore; that meditation had given me the ability to get to the root cause of the problem, and that we now had a real tool to help others suffering from anxiety, panic attacks, depression, PTSD, seizures, and who knows what else.

I called to schedule an appointment with Dr L, and before I knew it, Mom and I were on our way to his office. We were so excited, we were giggling and laughing all the way. Tears sprang to my eyes as I saw for the first time in eight years that the twinkle was back in Mom's eyes. I was filled with such overwhelming love and gratitude for this woman beside me. Here we were, mother and daughter, roommates and the very best of friends, enjoying ourselves and having a blast with the tunes cranked-up just like we used to. I was actually happy that the trip to Dr. L's office took us approximately 45 minutes, and I didn't mind at all the severe pain of sitting in the car for that length of time.

The closer we got to his office, the more excited I got. I just couldn't wait to tell him the greatest news ever, nor could I hide the huge grin on my face. His reaction would leave me shocked, bewildered and completely unsure.

Excitedly explaining my realizations, where they had lead, and the hope we now had for truly helping others, I must have gone on and on, completely oblivious to the change in Dr. L's facial expressions until he turned beet red and looked away. In anger and disgust, he loudly declared that I was completely delusional. I was taken aback, and so was Mom. He went into an angry tirade, feverishly spewing how going off the medications was the worst mistake I had ever made and one that I would soon regret. He went on to say that I had completely lost my mind and should be institutionalized. He then looked at my mom, and in an accusatory manner proclaimed that no mother would allow this to happen or go along with it.

We were there for what seemed like hours, being berated about the ridiculous choices I had made, where all this would lead, and that I would soon succeed in taking my own life. My head was spinning. I couldn't stand it for one more second, and turning away from him mid-sentence, I hobbled out and headed for the car. I soon felt Mom's arm reaching for mine, as she helped me the rest of the way. We drove home in silence, neither of us able to express what I believe we were both terrified of: that I had really lost my mind and was in a state of absolute delusion.

Diary Entry, October 2004

Am I delusional? Have I completely lost my mind? Is this just another suicide attempt beautifully disguised as a revelation? If this is insanity, then I love it, and I would rather be in this state than any other state I have experienced thus far. This is the first glimpse of light I've had since January 12th, 1996. How on earth can this be wrong? Maybe I am absolutely delusional and should be locked away in a straightjacket, as Dr. L so adamantly proclaimed.

I saw the twinkle in Mom's eyes, and the authentic laughter

we shared reverberates into my very being. I must be on the right track; I must be! Why is Dr. L so angry with me? Why was he so hurtful and vehement in his proclamations? I know he cares about me and always has my best interest at heart, so I just can't wrap my head around this.

I should listen to him and start taking the medications again, but just the thought of this makes my stomach turn. The thought of putting those pills in my mouth makes every cell in my body respond in protest. I am not taking those medications anymore, and I feel so much better since I stopped.

I will not allow anyone to change my mind about this. I will listen to the oh-so-obvious signposts telling me with every fiber of my being that I am on the right path. For the first time in almost nine years, I am on the right path. I can feel it. I'm excited and filled with such childlike curiosity! I can't wait to explore how much more I can discover with meditation and mindfulness. It feels like I am carefully turning the doorknob to a land never before explored. What will I see? What will I discover? I can't wait to find out.

What if this is the answer I've been seeking all along, and what if I could end up helping countless others suffering from debilitating diseases? Oh, I am willing to risk it all (and then some!) to turn that doorknob and walk into this unknown and somewhat frightening land, with just the slightest hope of discovery for all those suffering in silence. Yes! I am more than willing, and nothing is going to stop me. My feeling of excitement about this great adventure cannot be wrong. *(End of diary entry.)*

A few days later, sitting in Dr. B's office, I carefully detailed the discoveries I had made and their astonishing results, although my excitement was certainly subdued. Since the severity of the pain had decreased dramatically, I was down from 700mg to 480mg of OxyContin every twelve hours. I was able to walk Titus every day and thoroughly enjoy it. I was actually smiling again and not faking it. Mom and I were venturing out together and it was actually my idea every time. I was so happy to tell him that the panic attacks were gone, as were the seizures; that the depression and all of its horrible symptoms had lifted; that I could finally feel the sun again; and that I couldn't be more grateful.

As a deluge of thoughts regarding delusion and insanity flooded my mind, and with tears rolling down my face, I told him that this was all due to witnessing my thoughts without judgment or opinion, as well as daily meditation. Here were the words I so desperately needed to hear, and of course Dr. B was the one to deliver them: "I am so proud of you... and you never needed those medications anyway. You are my star patient and you never cease to amaze me. Would you be willing to speak with some of my other patients regarding pain management, dealing with tolerance, and what you've discovered?"

I don't know why I expected anything different from my hero. I guess it had been the shockingly unexpected reaction I received from Dr L just a few days prior. I can't begin to express how much I cherished this man and all he stood for. He was the most non-judgmental person I had ever met, with a mind so open and so willing that it was an honor just being in his presence. We achieved the results we were so desperately seeking, and he couldn't have been happier. He was excited and pleasantly surprised that our little meditation idea lead to all this, and he was hopeful for the future of chronic pain treatment.

Dr. B had taught me so much, and we had traveled quite the long and winding road together. But on this day he gave me the most precious gift of all—the permission to listen to myself first and foremost, without wavering, as well as to follow my joy in every instant for the utmost quality of life. Imagine quality of life being your number one priority... how can you make anything wrong when the sole focus or goal is quality of life? Thanks to Dr B, I had full permission to use "quality of life" as my measuring stick. As I looked up at this man sitting across from me, I couldn't help but hope that one day he would truly know how much he had done for me. As I was leaving, I walked around his desk and gave him the biggest hug. I wish everyone could be blessed with a Dr. B.

With renewed determination, I continued down the path of watching my thoughts and practicing meditation, while learning new tools to help me remain completely neutral and unfazed. This was fascinating to say the least; the discoveries were endless and mind-blowing.

The neck was still seizing, the hip made sitting at the kitchen table impossible, eating solid food was not an option, I still could not have a bowel movement without assistance, and the pain was debilitating. Yet everything had changed! With a perverted sense of amusement, I would watch the thoughts endlessly popping into my mind regarding all these circumstances, and I could see how ludicrous they were. They didn't have to be true unless I believed them.

This lead to a whole new epiphany. What if I redefined the word *pain*? Would the physical sensation change if I redefined physical pain? Changing the definition of pain from "hurt and suffering" to "loving messages from my body" would have to change how I feel and respond to it. But would it change the actual sensation? My experiment began and I was so excited to find out.

I had become a master at witnessing my thoughts, so in preparation for this new experiment , I wrote a few words about my new definition of pain. This was a word with a long negative history, and if I was able to change it to a positive definition, I couldn't fathom the implications. If I could actually achieve a different physical response, I could approach the medical industry and have them change their definitions. I was so excited! What did I want pain to be? A loving reminder of the present moment… yes, absolutely. A sense of awe regarding the physical form and all of its complexities, as well as its ability to send loving messages. Oh yes, I loved this! But the word *pain* carried so much heaviness on a collective level; I was sure I wasn't going to talk every doctor into removing the word from their vocabulary. So how could I literally redefine it? I had it, I had found the answer!

PAIN =

Physically
Accelerated
In
Non-resistance

This redefined the word for me, and also served as a reminder to not resist, but to lovingly remain in a state of surrender, with curiosity about deciphering its messages. Since I heard the word pain continuously by everyone in the medical industry and saw it written in all of the reports, I would be getting reminders constantly. I was excited to discover how my body would respond to this new definition. I began documenting the results, and they were shocking, to say the very least.

First and foremost, I was "leaning into" the pain instead of wincing or turning away from it. As if holding a precious child, I would surround the areas in pain with so much love and light. Eventually, this love and light filled my entire body. Images soon followed of the inside of my body being filled with beautiful beams of light in every color in existence and variances thereof, like sparkles. The areas of pain would always begin in darker shades, but soon they became as bright and beautiful as the rest of my body, and miraculously, the sensations would decrease dramatically, or even completely vanish.

I was flabbergasted. All that time spent in meditation, along with the visualization sessions filled with sparkles, had completely changed the *actual physical sensations.* How was this possible? How did anyone not know about this? How could I prove this? The thought of how many people this would help hit me like a ton of bricks.

There are no words to describe the magic that filled my every waking moment. Everything became a beautiful dance with meditation—from the witnessing of my arm lifting a cold glass of water, to the amazing sensations of the liquid permeating my mouth and continuing down my throat. The beautiful fragrances rising to my nose as I opened the cap of my favorite bubble bath... the tickles of the little hairs on my face rising in response to the hot water filling the tub... the feeling of the warmth caressing my skin as I slowly lowered myself into the water while noticing every little muscle responding in order to do so. How had I missed all this? How had I not noticed it before?

Never in my life had I experienced such magic. Or had I? As I noticed the tiny specks of light dancing ecstatically around me, I suddenly recalled that since my childhood, I had always seen these specks of light in nature, along with giant beams of white light emanating from the trees. I remembered that I called these tiny specks "mini fireflies" as a little girl, and a smile crept across my face. How had I let go of this magic? My brother and his wife had bought me a book called The Celestine Prophecy[2] in my early twenties, which had answered so many questions for me. I couldn't believe that I had completely forgotten the breathtakingly beautiful energy surrounding everything in existence and the healing wonders of nature.

Lying on a chaise in the backyard, I decided to pursue this passion even further. I closed my eyes and chose not to name or interpret any of the sounds that were so disturbing in our neighborhood. Our tiny little 12-by-10-foot backyard was adjacent to a police station. There was always traffic, sirens, voices and barking dogs. The airport wasn't far away and the sound of overhead planes was constant. We lived in a row of townhouses in a court that was filled with yelling neighbors, playing and screaming children, and loud thuds against the walls.

I took a few deep breaths, witnessing my diaphragm rising and falling as I emptied myself of every opinion, belief or judgment. With a childlike innocence, I listened to all of the sounds around me. Tears trickled down the sides of my face as this gifted choir orchestrated the most breathtakingly beautiful melody. Far off sounds of birds chirping in every tonal range joined in perfect harmony. The aliveness permeated every cell of my body as I listened to this exquisite performance. It filled my heart with an all-encompassing sense of pure awe and love.

There was one other thing I was extremely curious about and that was Post-Traumatic Stress Disorder (PTSD). Could this be cured with meditation and mindfulness also? I was certain it could. In 2004, I had seen yet another psychiatrist and had been diagnosed with PTSD, after I spent a year of suffering from memory flashes so debilitating that I would collapse onto the floor in a fetal position with bouts of violent vomiting. The memories were horrific and provoked a visceral reaction. The nightmares became so intense that I had to be medicated to sleep, and leaving the house had become impossible, due to severe anxiety and panic attacks.

Flashes of my forehead hitting the roof of the car, along with the impact to my body; flashes of the unknown driver stopping his vehicle after the accident to take a long look at the disaster he created before driving away; flashes of the scalpel gleaming when I awoke during surgeries and memories of the various sterile odors that permeated the room; flashes of needles being stabbed into every part of my body, and the sounds they would create as they went through bone; flashes of the experience in 2003 with the "doctor" and what took place in that examination room…

Even flashes of the sexual molestation I endured as a child returned to haunt me. I had been molested by a distant relative at the age of ten or so, which I only knew about due to my diaries, as I did not have access to the memories. Now the memories returned with a vengeance, along with all the gory details.

The nightmares I had were very graphic, waking me in a state of complete horror with so much sweat pouring out that Mom had to change my sheets. I didn't want to take the medications that were recommended for this, due to the awful reactions I had had to such medications in the past. But I had to do something. I certainly wasn't enjoying the debilitating feelings that accompanied each flash, so I decided to *change the memories*. I would keep track of all the memories that were coming back to haunt me and rewrite the storylines. A memory is indeed a thought, so if I could change a thought, then I could certainly change a memory.

The experiences themselves were long over, yet I was reliving them every single time they popped into my head or appeared in nightmares. I started visualizing the accident, and using my imagination, I would paste my preference of a beautiful dance in the Mustang that day, my body gracefully following the force of every motion. I even added a beautiful melody to this dance. Regarding the surgeries, the scalpels and the needles, I changed my focus to the surgeons, the nurses and their skillful hands taking such great care of me, mastering their craft. The experience with the doctor in 2003 was a little more challenging, due to my feelings of anger towards him. This made me realize that I was only hurting myself by continuing to carry these resentments. I wrote a letter telling him that I had completely forgiven him, and I thanked him for reminding me of how strong I was when I didn't even know it myself. I did the same with the little girl being molested—I rewrote the story. I walked into the room, lifted her off her abuser's lap, and while holding her in my arms, I got her out of there. I squeezed her tightly and told her she was safe, that she could let this go, and that I would protect her forever. I told her I loved her beyond words, that she was never alone, and that she was worthy of pure love; that she is pure love.

I was forced to confront my feelings of worthlessness and to learn unconditional self-love, and this had become a catalyst for change. It soon dawned on me that every person was a character in my play, in my story, and they had played their parts beautifully in my evolution. I thanked all of them for being a part of my transformation.

Every brutal scene in my memory became a beautiful dance, a co-creation filled with purpose and love. The unknown driver who caused the accident rolled his window down in concern but fled due to fear. I no longer judged him for that, and I felt nothing but love and gratitude. He taught me about true forgiveness and had been the catalyst for the greatest gift I'd ever received. This gift led to the emergence of the being who is writing this today.

I re-read the stories constantly and visualized the new scenes I had created. This soon resulted in a completely different reaction to the memory flashes. I would see the scalpel, but my attention was immediately brought to the surgeon's skillful hands gently caring for me as a smile crept across my face. Flashes of the accident changed into my body swaying to the melody and following the movement of the vehicle. The little Marie was safe, happily holding my hand as we skipped along side-by-side. The memories of the experience with the doctor no longer brought about feelings of shame or victimization; instead they were feelings of empowerment, and I hugged him for reminding me of how strong I was. I had rewritten history and reversed the debilitating symptoms of PTSD.

Diary Entry, June 2005

The magic... the magic is in everything. Without belief, opinion, judgment or label, everything is unfathomable and ungraspable. Every term I've been taught prevents me from truly knowing or experiencing the truth of existence—the truth of what I am. Sirens, loud voices, screaming children, thuds, traffic, and a deluge of other intrusive noises have become an angelic choir by emptying myself and becoming awareness itself.

Physical pain has become a privilege to witness. No longer is there a participant to label or complain about the sensations the pain is creating. This actually reduces the degree of the pain, or even resolves it entirely. Emotions no longer swallow me up. They have become my compass instead of something I dread. I see them as radiant signposts that point to whether I'm going in the right direction or not, just like I would automatically follow the signposts to get to a destination.

The anxiety, the panic attacks, and the horrible symptoms of PTSD have literally vanished. I am able to leave the house and interact with people without dreading the flashes of memories that used to completely paralyze me. I can actually go out in public now.

During meditation, the gaps of silence are becoming longer, and thoughts are becoming fewer and farther between. I was in meditation for over four hours yesterday, yet it felt like only seconds had passed. I witnessed my stomach inflate to the point of bursting, but the inhalations continued as my body effortlessly held its breath for what seemed like an eternity. There were tingling and firing sensations throughout my entire spine and nervous system, along with muscle twitches all over my body. The contortions in my throat, tongue, lips and diaphragm were crazy. I swear I was sitting up with my head tilted back, but my neck can't do that at all. What is this? If Mom was here, would she actually see movement? Or am I just imagining all of this?

I'm feeling so much better, but I have no idea why. This freedom, this bliss, and this unending and all-consuming sense of love is unexplainable. Yet here it is. The love I feel in each moment for everything and everyone... I can't even begin to describe it. As I lay here writing these words, tears are falling onto this very page and blurring the words. None of my circumstances have changed, yet my life is beyond magnificent in every way. I am so ecstatically happy and filled with so much love. My heart feels ten times too big. *(End of diary entry.)*

I didn't understand anything that was happening, but I reveled in the mystery of feeling so awesome without having any change in circumstances. My situation had remained unchanged, yet here I was, happier than a leprechaun in a field of four-leaf clovers. I loved everything, and I so thoroughly enjoyed meditation that I was excited as I went to sleep at night because I couldn't wait for morning to come so I could do it again.

This day was no different than any other, except that Mom had come home from work early to see what was happening. Let me tell you, when she saw me, she was panic-stricken and had the phone in her hand ready to call 911. She assumed I was having another seizure. I had said my usual mantra "I am" and had long been in meditation, when I felt my body sit up. It seemed that my stomach was inflating way over capacity while it held the breath. I must admit that fear struck, creating tension in my body as my head started falling backwards in slow motion. I emptied myself even more and relaxed, allowing my head to continue its journey. I couldn't believe what was happening, and I was sure there was no way it actually was.

All of a sudden, I heard Mom gasp in shock. My eyes flickered open to see the horror on her face and the phone in her hand. She yelled out, "Your head was laying on your back! I thought you were having a seizure. Marie, you looked like the girl in The Exorcist movie!" I giggled at the visual, and in complete disbelief, I turned my head in all directions, even flexing my neck backwards. There was not even a hint of resistance or pain. My shoulders were relaxed and not wrapped around my ears as I sat there completely bewildered. Mom rushed over to the bed asking if I was okay. I wrapped my arms around her, sobbing with sheer joy. She sighed in relief.

I had had no mobility in my neck since the accident, and as the years went on, despite countless needles, procedures and surgeries, it had only gotten worse. I had even had a massive needle full of botulism injected into my neck, right at the base of the skull. During this particular procedure, my head was resting on Mom's chest as she was standing in front of me, cringing at the thought of the excruciating pain this must be causing me. What she couldn't grasp (even though I had explained it to her many times) was that the pain was refreshing because it created a different sensation than the constant, unrelenting agony that was always present.

The injury that had caused me the most pain, the most debilitation, was gone. There was absolutely zero pain in that part of my body, as if it had never happened at all. Mom and I freaked right out, but it was gone nonetheless.

The inner voice that had been guiding me all these years roared with excitement, and of course as I always did, I wrote the messages down...

"You have finally gotten a glimpse of who you truly are, my beauty, and of what you are actually capable. You followed the excitement of no longer taking those medications, and you didn't allow the doubts, fears and obstacles to stop you. You discovered the bliss of manifestation.

I love you so much. I always knew you were hearing me; it is impossible not to. But now you're listening; hence this state of bliss. You're realizing that negative emotions are just loving signposts telling you that your thoughts are completely inaccurate and untrue. You're learning to use your built-in "navigation system," which we call "emotions," and I am so proud of you.

Everything you've been through has led to this. Every identity was stripped away from you so that you could discover the truth of what you are and what you have. The lack of self-worth and self-love was something you struggled with since you were a child. You know this. The accident just gave you the opportunity to face these things head-on and resolve them once and for all. You've experienced contrasts to the extreme, but see what it has brought and keep reminding yourself of this.

It's not about becoming anything at all. It's about unbecoming everything that life put upon you—everything you're not. Shed freely without labels and say Yes to the destruction. Allow what you've always been to rise from the ashes. You already are pure Divine Love; release the shadows and reveal your Self."

CHAPTER EIGHT

'My' Book?

If you can imagine those cartoon characters with the eyes bulging out accompanied by that "boing" sound... well, this was Mom every time I turned my head. That sound would come to mind resulting in a wild giggle fit. We couldn't understand or even begin to grasp what had happened, but we knew it was nothing short of a miracle. It had been a couple of months since I had done that exorcist-looking meditation, and I still hadn't even the slightest hint of pain or seizing in my neck. Yes, it was definitely a miracle!

I still had not received the reports from the independent examinations I had had almost three years before (in 2003), even though I had requested them countless times. This told me that something was up. On my claim representative's last day of employment with the insurer, he called to notify me that he was having the reports faxed to Mom's work, and that this was his act of going out in a blaze of glory. I so adored him and was sad to see him go, but I couldn't help but be extremely happy for him. I did not envy the position he held. I'd long realized that working for an insurance company and having to deal with cases like mine was heartbreaking. This afforded me much compassion for each and every claim rep in existence.

Mom arrived home from work with a thick white envelope in her hand, so I knew that he had succeeded in his mission. This put a huge smile on my face. After the endless excuses used in trying to keep these reports away from me, I couldn't wait to read them. I ripped open the envelope. There were thirteen questions asked by the insurer. These, of course, were answered by the doctors, along with reports of their diagnoses, prognoses and causation on the first few pages.

As I began to read the answers, along with their findings, tears poured from my eyes. From one report to another, their findings were conclusive and identical... well, at least the three I read. I didn't want anything to do with the monster doctor's report and threw it away upon opening the envelope. Just seeing his name made me cringe, and I was not going to subject myself to reading his words. I didn't care in the least what he had to say, anyway. Vacillating between sadness and anger, I eventually cried myself to sleep, with the reports still all spread out around me.

My mind was flooded with questions. Why the hell had I worked so hard to get copies of these stupid things? While reaching for my medication the next morning, I noticed the medical documents all neatly stacked on the table beside my bed in the living room. Mom's doing, of course. I couldn't help but wonder why these reports had hit me so hard. I had read hundreds of reports since the accident, yet these words had brought me to my knees.

First, these were independent examiners on behalf of the insurer, so I guess I expected some sugar-coating. These were their findings. The reason I was taking this so hard was because they not only stated my obvious current circumstances, but also listed their determinations and projections for the rest of my life. Line by line, answer by answer, they had written out in detail "my future" and everything that was to come.

Lying there waiting for the medication to take effect, I couldn't help but envision the future they had so clearly written out for me. What if this was my future? Who were these people—psychics who could predict the future with 100% accuracy? By this time, I knew how fleeting life was, so what if I was hit by a truck crossing the street today and was killed? That would certainly be a slap in the face to the grim prognoses they had made. Didn't I create my future by witnessing my thoughts in the present with neutrality, focusing on quality of life and believing in my dreams to such an extent that I knew they had already come true? Was this not a universal law called the Law of Attraction?

These documents stated that I didn't have a future and insinuated that I didn't have a purpose. I knew it was not true. I knew my purpose and had already made discoveries for helping others dealing with depression, chronic pain, PTSD, or any disease, for that matter. The thought of passing on this experience and paving the way for others lit me up in a way I had never felt before—not even policing, which had once been my biggest dream. I knew conclusively that circumstances had absolutely no power to prevent me from being in a state of blissful happiness, and that going deeper within myself had created nothing short of miracles. My purpose was to have the privilege of witnessing others expand their wings and fly, truly realizing they had never been caged in the first place.

Grabbing the stack of papers off the table, which included a copy of an email from Dr. L, I took a few deep breaths and began reading them again. But this time, I was the witness instead of the participant. Included below is only part of what the reports concluded and a combination of all the specialists' answers, but it's enough to give you the full picture:

> Ms. C's overall prognosis is poor, given her lack of improvement and recent regression in symptoms, despite extensive investigation and treatment. It is unlikely there will be significant improvement with respect to these symptoms, however, the coexistence of a mood disorder may be contributing to the severity of the physical symptoms. The diagnoses provided are not aggravation of a pre-existing condition. Her current medical treatment regimen is both medically reasonable and necessary, and will be ongoing indefinitely.
>
> Ms. C does suffer a complete inability to carry on a normal life as a result of the accident. Given the chronicity of

symptoms, the likelihood of any further medical recovery is quite low. Her level of functioning (occupational) is low but not due to psychiatric reasons. Ms. C's prognosis is contingent with the evolution of her physical symptoms, and therefore poor. Her depressed mood is secondary to the pain disorder, associated with a general medical condition.

A return to her pre-accident condition is highly unlikely. She has responded as well as one could expect, while the causes of her depressive mood—pain and diminished capacity to function—are unchanged. Further recovery in her depressive state is contingent to a very large extent on the evolution of her physical condition, and therefore poor. She should be closely monitored for suicide as she had already made an attempt. She will continue to suffer from depression with the primary cause being her physical condition. She will suffer from depression for the rest of her life."

I wondered what I would say to a friend if these were their reports. How would I help them see that, in fact, they create their experience as well as their future, and that swimming upstream was not necessary? How could I help them see that they can turn around at any time, and by allowing the current to carry them, enjoy one hell of a flight on soaring, beautiful thoughts?

As I visualized this friend, compassion and unconditional love filled every ounce of my being. Tears rolled down my cheeks as I realized this was exactly what I needed myself. To utterly and completely love myself unconditionally. To not take anything personally, knowing that everything is a signpost guiding my way. To focus on all the things I had to be grateful for, bringing so much more to be grateful for. To truly forgive myself and others by remembering that we are all extensions of each other, experiencing life from different perspectives. To drop all judgments, opinions and beliefs by reminding myself of the glimpses of light I had experienced, those profound periods of emptiness that were fulfillment beyond description. To remember... to remember... to remember my purpose, my calling, and the fire it created within me, along with the knowledge that it was already done.

Picturing myself speaking publicly about this journey and all the discoveries I had made along the way filled me with such joy, such love and such passion, that just the thought of it brought butterflies to my stomach. If I was going to help others remember what they are and always have been, then I should be remembering this myself.

I had been repeatedly told that I would suffer from depression and PTSD for the rest of my life, yet I had been free of symptoms and medications for over two years by not participating in my thoughts. The thoughts were still very much present (and sometimes relentless), but the oh-so-familiar emotional downward spiral no longer followed. Using my emotions as a navigation system, any negative feeling whatsoever was a reminder to return my attention to my thoughts and even write them down.

It was easy to see why I'd been feeling sad, as evidenced by the long list of self-deprecating thoughts that had been berating me. I couldn't help but laugh, knowing that these thoughts had no basis in reality. It seemed so simple that I couldn't comprehend how I had suffered so greatly for so many years. And because I had written about it every step of the way, it was all there in black and white. At the time, it would have been masochistic to go anywhere near those diaries, so I locked them up in the filing cabinet and forgot about them.

I was asked by Joan, a psychologist I was seeing in 2002, if I had done any journaling. I brought her everything I had ever written, even though I hadn't read any of it. Certainly this would have given me some insight into why I was so severely depressed. At our next appointment, I'll never forget her reaction after having read the 400 or so pages of my writings. She told me that she had just read the most profound book, from the most beautiful writer, and that this would someday be published. She told me she had not been able to put it down, that she was with me every step of the heart-breaking way, that she had felt every emotion, and that she knew this would reach many people.

Her words, albeit unbelievable at the time, sparked such curiosity and passion in me that I decided to put my diaries away for safekeeping, even as I continuously kept adding to them over the years. Little did she know that she had planted a seed that would break open even more of my purpose. I even started referring to the huge stack of papers locked away in the filing cabinet as "my book." I was an avid reader by this time, savoring each moment spent following some journey, but I couldn't imagine that someone would be reading my words someday! Joan's message echoed in my mind, abruptly putting a stop to any limiting beliefs regarding my book.

Mom thoroughly enjoyed bringing home all kinds of novels, as well as watching me lose myself as I turned the pages. I was not supposed to be able to process information or to have any short- or long-term memory, and at one point I had completely lost the ability to get through even a paragraph. So I'm sure she marveled at this miracle in front of her. She had come home with a little orange book tucked under her arm called A New Earth[3] by an author I had never heard of before, Eckhart Tolle. The book came highly recommended by our extraordinary friend, Sherrill. I must admit there were memory flashes of this very title jumping out at me throughout the last few months, and Sherrill's insistence made it impossible to ignore any longer. As I perused the headings of the chapters, my curiosity was certainly piqued. Totally unbeknownst to me, this book would change my life forever and provide the answers that had been eluding me my entire life.

From the book, A New Earth:

> A beggar had been sitting by the side of a road for over thirty years. One day a stranger walked by. "Spare some change?" mumbled the beggar, mechanically holding out his old baseball cap.
>
> "I have nothing to give you," said the stranger. Then he asked, "What's that you are sitting on?"

"Nothing," replied the beggar, "just an old box. I have been sitting on it for as long as I can remember."

"Ever looked inside?" asked the stranger.

"No," said the beggar. "What's the point? There's nothing in there."

"Have a look inside," insisted the stranger.

The beggar managed to pry open the lid. With astonishment, disbelief, and elation, he saw that the box was filled with gold.

I am that stranger who has nothing to give you and who is telling you to look inside. Not inside any box, as in the parable, but somewhere even closer—inside yourself.

"But I am not a beggar," I can hear you say.[4]

I was stunned! He was describing exactly what I'd been experiencing since Dr. B had encouraged me to give meditation a try. This state of peace, freedom and joy can't be explained or understood; it can only be appreciated and relished. Cover-to-cover in three days, and almost the entire book was highlighted in a multitude of colors. I had taken so many notes they could have easily filled a large bin.

The victim identity I had held onto for many years I could see without judgment, knowing that it was this thing called the "ego" or the "little me." It had absolutely nothing to do with what I was, and therefore it wasn't personal at all. I could also see all the times I had judged others, as well as myself, by the actions of the ego. By looking *through* the ego, for the first time I could experience what we all truly are and always have been. And to top it all off—the icing on the cake, the be all and end all—were the answers to the why's that had eluded me for as long as I can remember.

"Every experience is necessary for the evolution of your consciousness. How do you know this is the experience you need? Because this is the experience you're having at the moment."
~ Eckhart Tolle

I never again had to ask myself why all of this was happening because I trusted that it was necessary and for my highest purpose. I could release all attachment to my situation and circumstances by knowing they had no impact on my state of being, only my perception of them did. I also had the realization that this "little me" did indeed like to suffer, but that I was much more powerful than it could ever be.

What most excited me was that by using my emotions as a navigation system, I could remain in the highest vibration, regardless of circumstances. I could not only love the now, I could manifest all of my wildest dreams. Every reality already existed, and it was my choice to choose which one I preferred. It was that simple, and in hindsight, I had the power all along! It's just that I was looking everywhere but within, and that's the sole reason I couldn't find it. Just like the beggar in Eckhart's parable.

The privilege to not only feel the constant life force that animated my physical body, but to also have the ability to guide this peaceful, loving and healing entity after the depths of suffering she had gone through, was truly an act of sacred grace. The thoughts that had so tortured me were just old conditioned mind patterns. The tape playing was just in my head, conditioned by the past, by my ego (or my "pain-body" as Eckhart called it). I, the one behind the thoughts, the consciousness in which these thoughts existed, did not have to believe in them—and I hadn't in a very long time. The dread of what was to come vanished, and a state of peace and freedom washed over my entire body.

Diary Entry, February 2007

My ego feared being a failure, not being enough and being unlovable. Why fear? Because the ego arises from identification with form. Deep down, it knows that forms are not permanent, that they are all fleeting. There is always a sense of insecurity around the ego, even if on the outside it appears confident.

The truth of what I am... There is only one absolute truth from which all other truths emanate, and that is the truth of what I am. When you remember that truth, your actions will be in alignment with it. Human action can reflect the truth or it can reflect illusion.

People wouldn't be so afraid, skeptical or judgmental if they only knew that the energy flowing through their very Being is a phenomenal "wireless connection" to the most powerful source in the universe, God.

I am not religious (meaning I don't follow a certain set of beliefs within a dictated religion), but I have a deep and loving relationship with God, which is nurtured by the way I live. I thank God every single day for being with me, for loving me and openly receiving my love. I thank God for the countless blessings in my life, trust that everything is as it should be, and know that I am loved beyond anything I can imagine.

Others aren't wrong for not believing as I do, they are on their own journey. But underneath all the beliefs, judgments and opinions, we are all one; separation is an illusion. The discovery of my own essence has been the discovery of everyone's essence. We are truly one! God's love is pure, perfect and whole, and without judgment or bias. I must love as He does to know what love truly is. I am safe. I am loved.

Such a sense of complete acceptance and overwhelming freedom occurs when we don't want this moment to be any different than it already is; when we know that everything is already perfect and that we are loved unconditionally. Not even gratitude can incorporate all of the feelings of appreciation I feel for the Universe, for God, and for this sacred gift of Awakening.

Discovering Consciousness in myself and as myself is a journey of pure Divine Love, and it allows me to recognize every other as Consciousness, regardless of the actions of their human counterpart. Never in a million years could I have imagined this state of Being. I used to fill my days and evenings with television, figuring it was my only form of entertainment. What else was I going to do all day long? I didn't realize that stillness, just being with myself, was an option. I now appreciate this time immensely.

Meditation, stillness, creating space and being present have all become my priority. The teachings in A New Earth have drastically affected every aspect of my life. I have been waiting, asking God for these answers for a long time, and I can feel the difference in everything I am and everything I do. This inner peace, this outer peace, they pervade the core of who I am. I am Peace. This inner light, this outer light, they pervade the core of who I am. I am Light. I wasn't feeling love. But I am Love.

I am so grateful for the knowledge that I am not my thoughts. I am so grateful for this Consciousness arising in me. I am so grateful for the ability to feel, see, smell, touch and hear my inner body, my inner energy field. My body's intelligence is becoming aware of itself. The Consciousness that I Am is becoming aware of the life form of the body that it has temporarily evolved into. I am so grateful for the awareness that my primary purpose is to awaken, to realize that I have always been awake, and that awakening in itself is miraculous. I am so blessed to be alive.

Flashes of countless glimpses of enlightenment over the last few years flood my mind, and I am in complete awe of the many changes this has brought about. I keep wondering if these are "normal," but truly, why would they be? Living in full awareness and consciousness is totally new to me and to most other humans, is it not? So why would this be considered normal?

It is totally bizarre, but wonderful at the same time, to feel my body move by itself, as the muscles contract, expand and release; to hear the sounds of the breath being forcefully taken in to the point where it feels as if my stomach and ribcage will explode, and to then feel it slowly deflate to the sound of my outgoing breath. It was a challenge to allow this to happen without taking control. Now it seems to happen even when I'm not in meditation. I can sense this inner energy, breathing, tingling, and warmth most of the time. I sense it as an inner, loving, healing energy. All I truly recognize is that it is Love itself, and it feels awesome.

I see things differently, I feel things differently, and I am different. I thank God, the One that lives within, for every single thing and every single moment of my life, for it has all led me here, to this day and to this very moment. I wouldn't change this moment in any way. I wouldn't change this awakening process I am going through, nor the Truth that I am discovering myself to be. The Truth that I Am, and the Truth of what every single being on Earth is.

I've been wanting so badly for Mom to read A New Earth and to start meditating. I was telling myself that I wanted her to feel the kind of inner peace and sanctity that I feel, but that's not it at all—it is just more ego. My ego is judging her actions, non-actions and behaviors, strengthening itself by feeling superior. My ego is again wanting something from her; wanting her to read the book, wanting her to awaken, wanting her to change, wanting her validation. I now acknowledge those emotions and release them.

By seeing Mom with new eyes and detaching from the word *mom* itself, as well as freely sharing this loving energy with her, I've noticed a huge transformation. She has tons of energy, a super great mood and she's even mentioned a few times how wonderful she's been feeling. She's remembering her essence, what she truly is, in my love filled eyes and open heart. She is Essence, Sacredness, Consciousness, as am I.

She and I had a huge realization this week, which dumbfounded us. For our entires lives, we had unknowingly been putting people up on a pedestal, and when they failed to meet our expectations, we would feel hurt and betrayed. We had been creating our own suffering by having expectations of others and placing responsibility onto them, instead of remembering that we were already complete and limitlessness. We had been completely blinded to the person's sacred being by defining them in some way or wanting them to be different.

Experiencing life and all its contrasts is so much fun with Mom. We can always tell one another we're full of shit without taking offense, because we know that we actually are. And we laugh hysterically in the process.

Of course living together as adult women, we can drive each other crazy sometimes. There are small perceived resentments that the ego would love to turn into monstrous grievances, if left to its own devices. We've come up with a "magic phrase" we use to defuse any ego attacks between us and prevent our pain-bodies from mutually energizing each other. "MOM I LOVE YOU - MARIE I LOVE YOU." This swiftly does the trick. We each know what the other means, and due to the relationship we've always shared, this stops the ego in its tracks with an instantaneous return to love.

The same applies to my lifelong judgments and expectations with my brothers and my father. The ego in me, the "little me," wants approval, validation and love from them. I acknowledge these emotions and set them free. Each one of them is Essence, Sacredness, and Consciousness. As am I.

As I sit here thinking of all the perceived atrocities in the world, I realize that it is absolute insanity to create suffering for myself and others by allowing the "small me" to get upset and disturbed when it seeks security and fulfillment in transient things—and obviously fails to find it. I create suffering for myself and others whenever I make anyone or anything wrong in order for me to be right. This has the opposite effect of my highest passion and purpose: for people to remember what they truly are.

The feelings that have arisen certainly cannot be described as subtle. They are abundant and magnificent, and never in a million years could words do them justice. I feel overwhelming gratitude, peace and love for the privilege of picking up the neighborhood garbage, consisting of dirty decomposed diapers, feminine pads, pizza boxes, etc. I relish the hours spent raking and cleaning out my yard, when not too long ago, my ego would have been too busy complaining, blaming and using "why bother" excuses to do anything. This only strengthened the ego by making others wrong in order to be right. I used to be too identified with my "victim role" and too consumed by "my pain" to realize I could actually enjoy these things.

Tears are streaming down my face due to the overwhelming love, peace and connection I feel for the entire Universe, for life, for God. I am just so grateful after completing these seemingly simple tasks. Recognition is no longer required, no longer necessary. The thanks is all mine for this wonderful life, for this exquisite present moment, and for this incredible Being that I Am.

I am madly in love with the present moment, in all the splendor of its presentations. I am the stillness that accepts it as it already is. I refuse to judge or to make anything wrong, so I can light up the world and everyone in it. The illusion that I am separate from the power that runs the universe has ultimately dissipated. I now fully remember what I am, always have been and always will be. To share this state of being and to serve as a reminder is my sole purpose for existing. To look into the eyes of another and recognize the truth of what they are... there are no words. But it is my life's mission that people experience this.

Life is so incredibly giving—either way, negative or positive. But without a perceiver, there are just contrasts. In my case, life has been incredibly beautiful and I am eternally grateful. I am so blessed to have been given the path to surrender, and to every path it has led me to since. I am also grateful for the resistance and the struggle, for I would not be where I am now without them. How could I possibly label or complain about anything that has happened when it has led to this outcome? I know this is the inevitable outcome of any suffering.

Suffering was not a punishment, it was a gift that served as a reminder of what I truly am. Suffering is beautiful; its sole purpose for existence is to lead you back to God, the One, your Self—to the remembrance of what you truly are. There is an inevitable limit to suffering, where this discovery is certain. How miraculous!

God, I love you! I feel you in everything that I do and everything that I am. Thank you for the countless blessings in my life. What more could I possibly ask for? *(End of diary entry.)*

This sense of peace was abruptly interrupted by a few new symptoms that I had not experienced before, and I couldn't help but be a little freaked out by their intensity and bizarreness. There were spasms in my right leg, which I was all too familiar with due to the bone cysts and scar tissue in the hip, but they were associated with a feeling of numbness and tingling, almost like tickling inside the leg. I would constantly rub the leg, since it was driving me crazy, and Mom soon noticed. The symptoms progressively got worse, worrying us both. Since Dr. B had returned to the Armed Forces and was no longer my doctor, there was no choice but to look for another doctor. This proved impossible. There was no doctor willing to take me on as a patient, although we contacted and met with many doctors in our area and the surrounding regions. I was beyond terrified, and I grew more desperate by the day, as did Mom. What was happening?

The inner voice persisted....

"Marie, remember this state of being and everything you've discovered. Remember your purpose and the fire it lights up within you. Print this last diary entry, have it framed and put it up on the wall beside your bed. Remember that you are not separate from the power that runs the universe.

I'll never leave you and I will remind you of what you truly are, every step of the way. Notice the signposts and use your emotions as they are meant to be used, as a navigation system. There will be doubts, challenges and obstacles, but don't let them deceive you into forgetting. Any way you choose to live this, I'll love you through it as always, and will be here to see you through. You're going to believe that this is more than you can take, but I'm here to tell you that it is not. Listen for me, my beauty. You are safe. You are never alone. You are loved."

CHAPTER NINE

Worse Than Ever?

What I would go through in the next eighteen months would make the last twelve years pale in comparison. I would even go as far as to say that everything I had experienced thus far couldn't even approach the depths of physical torture I was now facing. I was completely bedridden 24 hours a day, and lost every physical ability, including the capacity to be touched in any way whatsoever. Even the slightest brush against my skin would send my entire body into a frenzy of torturous and unbearable symptoms resulting in panic, screams, tears and desperation. Although I wrote nothing during this almost two-year period, I remember it all too well. The symptoms began innocently enough, however, they soon worsened to the point of insanity.

The mediation for my insurance claim was scheduled for October of 2008 in Toronto, a four-hour drive, and I had no clue how I was going to make it in this condition. I almost cancelled. Mary, my lawyer's assistant, encouraged and pushed me to not miss this mediation, since the trial date had already been set to begin the following month in Sudbury, Ontario. The trial would be much more intensive than a one-day conference.

Mom set up the car, turning it into a patient transport so I could lie down. Still, it was the most excruciating four hours of my life. The realization that I was dying came over me during that ride and I knew exactly what I had to do. The mediation had been arranged in a conference room on the main level of a hotel;

we were staying in a room on the second level. I pushed with everything in me to put on some dress pants and a blouse, which were now hanging off me due to weight loss. I grabbed the thick white belt of the hotel robe and secured it around my pants to hold them up, letting the blouse hang over the top. I could do this and I had to.

Listening to my wonderful lawyer, Ivan, I was filled with hope for Mom's future. As I caught sight of Mary, the woman who had been fighting for me for the last two years since Ivan had taken over my case, my eyes teared up with an overwhelming sense of love and appreciation. Mary was the most caring, compassionate and loving woman, and she was the best in her field because of it.

Mary constantly went to bat with the insurance company on my behalf, not accepting the outrageous manner in which we were living. She made them pay for a commode so that I could pull myself out of bed and sit on an actual toilet, instead of having to use a bed pan when Mom was home (or urinating the bed when she wasn't home). She knew every detail of our lives, she listened attentively and asked questions. Mary made living much more bearable for Mom and me. Although Mom had to carry the heavy urine-filled basin up a fight of stairs to empty it into the toilet, this was much better than coming home to find her daughter soaked in urine. I reached out to give Mary the biggest hug, despite what this gesture was going to do to my body.

Sitting in that room on a chair, I could feel my heart pounding uncontrollably. I thought I was going to die right there in front of all these strangers. As hard as I tried to take deep breaths to slow down my racing pulse, it just kept speeding up until the sound of the pounding deafened me. The room began to spin and I was sweating profusely. I began shivering, and I leaned over to whisper in Mom's ear, "I have to go back to the room." Her eyes widened. This mediation was what we had been waiting for, and after this 13-year fight, I was leaving?

I had spoken often of what I'd say to the insurers when I finally got the chance. The opportunity was at hand, yet I was leaving. She knew instantly that I was not doing well at all; that this was serious. As I left the room, I looked back at her dread-filled eyes. In that moment, I truly didn't know if I would see her again. I have no recollection of making my way to our room or how I got there. The only memory I have is of being face down on the bed, fully clothed. I vaguely recall hearing Mary's voice, but I have no idea what was said. I believe she was checking on me, but to this day, I don't know what words were exchanged, if any. I only remember her voice.

I woke up frozen to the bone, shivering like a leaf. I slowly began to remove my wet, sweat-soaked clothing, beginning with untying the belt of the robe I had wrapped around my waist. My pants fell to the floor. Everything was a haze as I put on my warm pajamas and wrapped my thick housecoat around me. I carefully arranged the pillows to hold me up in a reclining position. This brought me comfort, and I soon began to feel a bit better. I grabbed the little hotel notepad on the bedside table and wrote down everything that was in my heart in that moment:

God, just take care of Mom. That's all I care about. You and I know I'm coming to be with you soon, and she at least deserves to have the financial burden of the last thirteen years lifted off her shoulders. She also deserves to have a home without payments, a good reliable car so she can visit our family, and money in the bank to facilitate all this. She's going to need my brothers, God, and she's going to need her siblings too—without the worry of how to pay for all this. We both know there is no need for anything where I'm going, so just take care of her until she joins me. This is all I ask.

I wondered how the mediation was going, and I brought my hands up to pray as I read my little note. Within the next hour, Mary returned to quickly discuss the insurer 's first offer. It was much higher than I'd expected as a starting bid, and I knew that my prayers had been heard. Although Mary was cautious, I knew what this meant.

The negotiations continued until it was time for a lunch break. Mom and Mary came to the room to spend some time with me. I have no recollection of anything that was said, but the look of worry and despair in Mom's eyes shook me to my very core. Did she know I was dying? I had to fight, to hold on with everything I had... for her. Since I was feeling better, I returned to the conference room. The next thing I remember is the final offer being made. I looked over at Mom and asked if it was okay with her. I didn't care about money whatsoever at this point, therefore I was definitely not in a position to judge the number in front of me. This was her call. She nodded in agreement of the offer, and that was the end of the negotiations.

I signed off on the papers with Ivan by my side. He placed a blank piece of paper on the table in front of us and wrote the settlement amount at the very top of the page. On the left side of the page he began writing the amounts of our accumulated medical debt, the approximate cost of our dream house, furnishings, medical equipment, vehicle, future rehabilitation costs and anything else he could think of. He calculated the total of these numbers, then subtracted this amount from the settlement proceeds, leaving the amount he would take for his fees. Considering what he was entitled to, this number was utterly insignificant.

I saw in that moment what Ivan was truly made of and wept with a deep sense of love and gratitude. It took my breath away. He had worked feverishly to settle this claim in two years, bringing some closure to Mom and I after such a long and brutal battle, and he deserved every penny he was entitled to. He was choosing to ensure that our needs were met entirely, and that the financial burden would be lifted from Mom. I loved him dearly for everything he had done, and as I sit here writing these words, tears fall as I recall his selfless act of pure love.

I was then approached by the insurer's lawyer, a stunning and sharply-dressed lady in her fifties. She was escorted by a beautiful woman whom I soon realized had been my claim representative for the past few years. The lawyer told me that I was not what she expected; that I was articulate, well-mannered and legitimately disabled. She profusely apologized for the long, drawn-out fight, and I could see that she was being sincere. Looking at her in that moment, all I could feel was compassion. As I offered my hand to hold hers, I hoped that she would never again judge a book by its cover; that she would remember this moment and would not ever repeat such treatment with another.

The claim rep then asked if I had any outstanding receipts for treatment or medications from the last two weeks. The claim was settled, it was over, yet here she was taking out a checkbook to cover anything that had not been included in the claim. I was touched, and I knew that this had been a profound awakening for them both. Upon lovingly saying our goodbyes, I filled them with every ounce of love and light within me.

The annuity firm specialist had been present for the mediation. He came into the room to explain the settlement in detail, and to discuss options and recommendations for dealing with this amount of money. He had been hand-picked by my lawyer, so I knew his knowledge was unsurpassed and I trusted him implicitly. We made some decisions we were both satisfied with, and agreed to continue to run numbers once I was home.

Upon hearing the word *home*, the thought of the four-hour ride made me shudder in fear. I knew I had to suck it up and fight... for Mom. I couldn't leave her; I had to fight with everything I was.

I didn't understand what was happening with my body, nor did Mom. Our search for answers had grown desperate, and had led us once again on a wild goose chase. I was at the point where I could only open and close my eyes. The last of my attempts to stand had abruptly come to a stop. I was trying to grab my water bottle off the end table when my legs gave out. I fell, smashing my rib cage into the open drawer and cracking my jaw as it hit the glass top. I broke three ribs. I was on the phone with Dr. L at the time, and the phone flew out of my hand. To this day, I have no idea how he got to our house so quickly.

There was no escaping what was occurring in my body. Even turning my head to watch television or attempting to focus on my breath was impossible due to extreme, constant and horrific spasms. Because of the broken ribs, the pain was unbearable each time I took a breath. It felt like a million snakes had burrowed inside every inch of my body, constricting each muscle, ligament and bone, then releasing for an instant before continuing the constriction. Mom could see the muscles in my legs, hips and lower abdomen pulsating, vibrating, popping and tensing until I screamed in agony.

Mom did everything in her power to help me through this. She would repeatedly play this one song called The Climb[5] by Miley Cyrus, with the volume cranked all the way to ten, knowing this was the only thing that would bring me out of this terror. I would listen focused on every word, and as tears poured from my eyes, I would scream at the top of my lungs with every lyric. Just remembering the lyrics to this song makes me cry as the melody plays in my head. In an instant it brings back all the feelings of what this song meant to me then, and still does now.

Mom inflated a special air mattress bed that circulated the air regularly to help prevent bedsores, and that's where I stayed. I was dressed only in hospital gowns and I didn't move for anything. I would get cold and ask her to put a light sheet over me, but soon I would be screaming in a panic for her to take it off. Anything even slightly touching me would cause the spasms to intensify and spread throughout my entire body, getting closer and closer to my heart. It felt like I had no access to breath, and that I was literally being crushed from the inside out.

Mom would run over as fast as she could, rip the sheet off, sit on the floor beside me and kiss my nose as I tearfully yelled at her, "If you loved me, if you really loved me, you would kill me. You would never be able to sit by and watch me get tortured like this every second of every day. You would put me out of my misery and do what I did for Judge and for Titus out of complete love." She couldn't wipe my tears or hold hers back any longer as they rolled down her cheeks. The look of utter devastation in her eyes ripped my heart to pieces as we both sobbed uncontrollably, without the ability to hold and comfort each other. I was lying on the air mattress while Mom sat on the floor beside me, careful not to even brush against the mattress. I reached out my hand to hold hers whimpering, "I'm sorry. I'm so sorry, Mom. I know how much you love me and I love you too... so much."

She desperately wanted to feed me, but the years of pureeing yams and spooning them into my mouth were long gone. I could only tolerate juice from a straw, and only in tiny amounts. I can't even begin to imagine the helplessness she must have felt having to watch her only little girl slip further away every single day. I was transported to every doctor's appointment by ambulance or patient transport, and we lost count of the hospital stays. The diagnosis of MS was being thrown around, but the main focus was always on the symptoms and the attempt to relieve them even slightly. But it was to no avail.

The nurses and personal support workers visited daily until I could no longer deal with anyone but Kate, who was my favorite nurse. She created the most ridiculous avatar on my Wii video console and would make it do all kinds of things to make me laugh. She would walk in and stand beside my bed, teasing me for crying yet again. She called me a big cry baby, which would actually provoke a spontaneous giggle through my endless tears. Kate would check my bedsores and deal with them with such a gentle touch that I could hardly feel it. She would go on and on about how pitiful I was, making me giggle loudly. I cherished and appreciated her with all my heart.

Dr. L came to the house at every opportunity, and as Mom carefully lifted me into a sitting position, he would inject epidurals into my lumbar spine, providing some relief from the bone cysts in my hip, the disc protrusion and degeneration, the annular tear at L5 S1, and the bedsores. Immediately after the injection, I had to return to a prone position, which caused much fright on a few occasions. After the injection, I felt my diaphragm and rib cage becoming numb, and let Dr. L know that I was having trouble breathing. I had never seen him jump so quickly! Without a thought of gentleness, he yanked me up as if I was a rag doll. In layman's terms, the medication was traveling in the wrong direction, upwards towards my lungs, which obviously could kill me. I didn't flinch at the thought of it, and I pondered whether I would tell him the next time or just keep my mouth shut. What a beautiful way to die! But Mom... I had to think about Mom.

An ambulance was called yet again, this time by Sherrill, who had been staying with me that morning, since I couldn't be left alone. I remember suddenly opening my eyes and looking at her in terror, mouthing the word "ambulance." The look on her face flashes in my mind as I write this. The medics arrived instantly it seemed. They put a shot of nitroglycerin under my tongue, a cuff on my arm and a little clamp on my finger to monitor my heart rate and oxygen levels.

This had become such a regular occurrence that I guess they were accustomed to it and knew exactly what to do. I would quickly be moved to the stretcher, wrapped in blankets. I would scream about the weight of the blankets and vehemently refused to be strapped in, as I could hear my heart rate skyrocketing. Another shot of nitro and I was in the ambulance on my way to the hospital.

Screams came out of me with every bump and movement. There were five speed bumps from our townhouse to the end of our court, plus four more to get to the street. The ambulance had to turn around and run over all nine to get out to the street. Why didn't they turn around before parking in front of my house to attend to me and avoid this all together? Although I pondered this often, I already knew the answer: there was absolutely no time to waste in getting to me.

In the heart ward at the hospital, there were machines all around me, and countless wires and tubes sticking out of me. The massive amount of morphine and OxyContin in my system finally took effect. I looked into Mom's exhausted eyes and told her to go home. She refused, shaking her head from side to side. I finally talked her into getting some rest, reassuring her that I would be just fine surrounded by competent professionals. I even went so far as to tell her I preferred that she to go home so I could finally get some sleep after five sleepless nights in a row. We had both been awake for six consecutive days, and we both desperately needed sleep. As I drifted off to sleep, I felt her hand slip away from mine. I hoped I'd get to see her again, one last time.

"Marie, don't make me bag you. Breathe Marie, breathe! Don't make me bag you!" These words pierced through my slumber as I gasped for breath while all of the machines around me beeped loudly. This happened several times throughout the night. I can still remember in vivid detail my eyes popping open to see the white ceiling above me. I can still hear the nurse's frantic voice echoing in my ears to this day.

I have no recollection of anything during those 40 hours or so, except that the torturous and relentless spasms somehow seemed further away. I could still feel everything, and nothing had changed, but it was all a fog and I wasn't able to speak at all. I remember two nurses, the one who had been caring for me and one I didn't recognize, standing beside my bed looking down at me and then over to the machines. I remember hearing the words *morphine, breathing, oxygen levels* and *bagging*, but that was about it.

I knew I was being given 10cc of morphine every hour, as this was the dose they injected into my intravenous line upon arrival. I couldn't understand what this meant. I also remembered the 480mg of OxyContin being administered every 12 hours by mouth. I have no recollection as to who was administering this, but it must have been Mom. I had been on this dosage for many years, and she obviously knew exactly what would happen if the dose was missed... and she ensured that it wasn't.

I could hear Mom's voice speaking loudly to the doctor, the nurses and anyone within ear shot, but I couldn't make out a single word as I was fading in and out. The last memory I have of this hazy odyssey was of the new nurse putting only 5cc of morphine into my drip every 30 minutes, instead of 10cc every hour. A sense of horror filled my entire being, as I instantly knew that I would soon be face-to-face with the full impact of my symptoms. I slipped away once again, unable tos peak in protest.

I awoke to Mom 's hand gently but firmly holding mine, as if holding on for dear life. I knew this hand, every inch of it, and without even opening my eyes, an overwhelming sense of pure love permeated my very being. I was given the chance to see her again, and upon opening my eyes, there she was. Tears streamed down both our faces as our eyes met with such love; such pure, unconditional and unwavering love. I had to keep fighting. I had to keep pushing. I had to hold on; I couldn't give up. This woman looking back at me has never given up on anything in her entire life, and would never even conceive of giving up on me.

The recognition in that moment was beyond explanation. It was as if there was a mirror and I was looking at myself. There were no longer two of us in a hospital surrounded by machines and nurses; there was only me. In that moment, I felt the entire universe itself. The thought that I had never given up on anything in my entire life, and certainly wouldn't conceive of giving up on myself, blazed through my mind, replenishing my spirit and giving me the will to fight.

The first words I was able to utter were, "Mom, don't let me die like this. I don 't want to die in a hospital while unconscious. I want to be awake and with you at home. Call Dr. B, Mom; his cell phone number is in my contacts. Let me speak with him." Before I knew it, Dr. B's reassuring voice was on the other end of the line. To hear his voice after all these years, and knowing him as I did, I had no doubt that he would make everything better.

After explaining what was happening and what lead up to it, he asked me to hand the phone to the doctor on duty. I called out to the doctor on duty and passed the cell phone over to him. The look of surprise on his face was unmistakable as he took the phone out of my hand and proceeded with a friendly hello. They obviously knew each other.

Immediately following the conversation, the doctor returned to my bedside with a syringe and explained Dr. B's recommendations. I could finally breathe a sigh of relief knowing that whatever Dr. B had advocated, it would work. He knew me well and had been there since the beginning.

The doctor injected 2mg of Diazepam into my intravenous line. Soon afterwards, I sat up sobbing in disbelief, as the symptoms had completely vanished. This was the first time in almost two years that I didn't feel like I was literally being crushed from the inside out. Mom was standing beside the bed with tears in her eyes. I jumped to wrap my arms around her, telling her she could finally wrap hers around me. Without hesitation, we held each other and wouldn't let go. I breathed her in for what seemed like forever, buried in her chest and crying from sheer joy and relief. There simply are no words to express how it felt to be in Mom's arms again.

Just 2mg of Valium, or Diazepam, had removed my pain. How was this even possible? I didn't understand it in the least, but I appreciated the relief beyond description. I remembered the doctor reiterating what Dr. B had explained—that if we could control the muscle spasms we could control the pain. But 2mg of Valium compared to 10cc of morphine? Dr. B was going after the actual muscle spasms themselves, instead of the pain they were causing. How brilliant! I knew he would have the answer.

I was soon moved out of the heart ward and into a room in another ward. I was prescribed 2mg of Diazepam every six hours. As my bed was being pushed down the hallway, a smile appeared on my face as I looked up at Mom.

I was in my new room with five other patients when panic struck me. I could feel the spasms and contractions returning. I looked at the clock and realized it had been six hours since my last dose. I pressed the help button repeatedly for over thirty minutes until a nurse appeared with a needle, stuck it in my upper arm then walked away. This describes the next three days, until I demanded to see the doctor.

I had been reassigned to another doctor, whom we'll call "Dr. Marten." I won't repeat what Mom called her (and still does to this day). The nurses had repeatedly tried to change the Diazepam injection from "PRN (when necessary), maximum every six hours" to "automatically administered," so it could be added to their rounds. But the doctor wasn't having it. I gave her Dr. B's cell phone number as she proceeded to berate me, stating that the fact that Diazepam relieved my symptoms was proof that this was all in my head. She said I was causing myself all this suffering due to anxiety, and that she was not under any circumstances going to call a specialist at home on a weekend. She told me to suck it up and deal with it, and that she didn't want to hear from me again.

I hadn't allowed myself to sleep at all since I had been put in that room, as I was in absolute fear of sleeping past the six hours, missing the Diazepam injection and waking up in an outright nightmare of torture again. I was unable to have the head of the bed elevated, due to the bone cysts in my right hip, the disc protrusion and degeneration, and the annular tear at L5-S1. So I remained completely flat on my back, staring at the clock on the wall, watching the seconds tick by for hours on end, until it was time to press the help button again.

The smell of food would fill my nose as the cafeteria staff would roll the giant shelved units down the hallways and into the rooms as they robotically placed the trays on each patient's table. With my peripheral vision I could see my food tray. I so desperately wanted the juice and the applesauce, but I was completely unable to roll onto my side to grab anything. I tried using the curved end of my cane, but the food and juice just fell to the floor, frustrating me to the breaking point.

A woman caring for her mom in the bed across from mine walked over, picked up the juice, opened it and placed the little straw inside before handing it to me. I swear, I drank it all in one gulp. She then bent over and grabbed the apple sauce, ripped it open, dipped the spoon, filling it to capacity and carefully put it into my mouth. The taste of that applesauce was divine, and I savored every spoonful until it was all gone. She then walked over to her mom's tray, picked up the juice and the applesauce and returned to feed me once again.

She told me that her heart was breaking watching me just lay there for the past few days, but she didn't want to come any closer to me, since she was certain her mom had a very contagious skin disease. She was a nurse and had been arguing with Dr. Marten to put her mom in isolation since bringing her to the hospital, but again, Dr. Marten would not budge. As tears welled up in her eyes, she continued to feed me the applesauce. She told me that she couldn't stand it for one more second; she had to come over to give me something to drink and eat. She took every precautionary measure possible to prevent me from catching her mom's disease.

Tears now falling down her cheeks, she expressed how seeing my mom and I together every night reminded her of the relationship she and her mom shared. She also confessed that my mom had confided in her about how hard it was to continue working, as she couldn't be here with me during the day. As I looked up into those beautiful eyes, I couldn't have felt more grateful for this act of grace or have been more deeply in love with this being standing above me.

The six-hour mark was quickly approaching, and by this time, I knew pressing the call button thirty minutes prior was the only way to ensure that the medication's effect wouldn't wear off before I received the next dose. A young male Asian nurse was beside me in moments. He gasped in horror and put his hand over his mouth. My arm was really sore, but I had no idea why—and this pain was nothing compared to the pain in the rest of my body. He said to me, "You poor sweetheart! Look at you. How could this have gone on for so long? A butterfly needle should have been put in days ago." He rushed away and quickly returned with a butterfly needle. Soon he had it in place and reached for the syringe to inject the Diazepam. I didn't feel a thing, which was refreshing.

Mom showed up a short while later and announced that Dr. B had taken care of everything. I no longer had anything to worry about; they were busting me out of this place! The medics came into the room and moved me onto to the stretcher. I was finally going home. Like I've said countless times, I would not be here without

Dr. B. Even though I hadn't been his patient for years, he still went to the ends of the earth for me. As I was being transported home, I couldn't help but tearfully think of Dr. B and all he had done for me. I felt so immensely blessed.

The Reveal

"How I wanted to lift her out of that wheelchair all those years ago and go through everything for her since the very beginning. I wanted to show her the way, give her strength and love her beyond anything she could fathom. I wanted to lift her out of that bed, hold her in my arms and tell her she had nothing to worry about because I had her and would never let her fall. I wanted to carry her every step of the way.

I guess I did, because this is my story and this happened to me. My name is Tina Marie Blackwell (formerly Corriveau), and this is indeed my story.

We all have a higher self, a higher power, as did I. The woman I am today is not the girl I was in 1996, although in every moment, I had full access to the strong inner voice and indomitable spirit of the being I am and have always been. We all do, and nothing we do can change that. It took a long while and much suffering for me to remember what I truly am, but I couldn't be more grateful that I was given every chance, was shown every signpost leading the way, and had caught beautiful glimpses along the journey.

The words I wrote at the end of each chapter were part of my awareness every step of the way, but I did not want to hear or even acknowledge them until I dropped the victim identity, stopped taking cues from my circumstances and opened my heart to the guidance available to me. I continued to push away everything other than my pain. In my pain I was comfortable; it was familiar. I didn't want to let go of victimhood. Facing my own death forced me to step out of my personal, self-inflicted hell, making me realize that I had never been alone, that this love was available to me at every moment and that I had the power all along.

Marie died that day and Tina was born. I am Marie. I am Tina. I had been playing both characters since the very beginning. I was the victim stuck in what seemed like a never-ending torturous life, but I was also the higher self, holding the victim's hand. I heard the guidance all along, since I am still here to tell my story."

CHAPTER TEN
The Gift of Death

By this time, I fully understood what had occurred in the heart ward and the meaning of those frantic words, "Don't make me bag you, Tina - breathe!" The principle of *double effect* refers to the ethical construct in which a physician uses a treatment, or gives medication to a terminally ill patient for an ethical, intended effect. The intended effect is to relieve the patient's pain, but the secondary effect is that it will almost certainly hasten their death. I was so far gone, why wouldn't the doctors go all in?

Due to the extreme tolerance I had built up to narcotics, the "intended effect" required much larger doses than a typical person would require. My oxygen levels were constantly dropping as I literally could not remember to breathe. It wasn't even part of my awareness, and due to the morphine's relaxing effect on the muscles surrounding the lungs, and the OxyContin's respiratory depression, breathing was no longer an automatic function. The nurse's frantic screams were to provoke enough consciousness to make me take a breath. If I hadn't, I would have been intubated (bagged).

There had been no investigation into the cause of what was happening with my body nor did there seem to be any interest in finding one. This lead me to believe that nothing much could be done except for symptom management. I knew by the green color of my skin that my organs were struggling, but why the full-body muscle spasms? Was it Multiple Sclerosis, as suggested repeatedly by several doctors or was it something else?

The multitude of trips to the hospital and the countless stays always had the same outcome—symptom management. Lying at home in the living room, I realized how close I had come repeatedly to never seeing my mom again or even getting to say goodbye. Though I knew that time was soon approaching, as I could feel my life-force fading by the minute, at least we would be together now that I was home. We would share whatever days I had left and enjoy each other's company. It was a relief that I was fully conscious and that the relentless, torturous symptoms were being fully controlled by Diazepam. I took a deep breath, fully exhaling as if I hadn't in the last two years. I peacefully drifted off to sleep without even a thought about having to press a help button. I was home with Mom, where I belonged.

I awoke to Mom stroking my cheek with the back of her hand, which instantly put a smile on my face. I knew that hand, every inch of it. I opened my eyes to catch Mom adoringly looking at me as tears rolled down her face. She was the strongest woman in existence. This was the second time I had seen her cry in the past couple of years, though I often heard her sobbing into her pillow at night. Knowing how hard she was trying to conceal her pain and how much she needed to remain the strong one, I never mentioned it. I lifted my arms to take her into an embrace as she ever so gently laid her head on my chest. How I loved this woman! How I cherished this woman! How blessed I was to have the privilege of calling her Mom. I told her that everything was okay now, that we could just focus on each other and forget everything else.

My cousin Danielle came to visit that day and I was so happy to see her. She had visited often while living in Ottawa and even more so in the last couple of years. After her diagnosis of ALS (Lou Gehrig's Disease) a couple of years prior, I had challenged her to go to Sedona, Arizona and have a guide bring her to one of the vortexes. She didn't believe in a higher power, or at least had never felt a connection. I so wanted her journey through ALS to be one of love, surrender and faith. I told her I would never again speak to her about spirituality if she would spend some time in the vortex and tell me she felt nothing. I would love her through her journey, regardless. She had taken me up on my challenge.

Upon her return, she was sitting in the Lazy Boy in my living room chatting with Mom, and as I woke from my slumber our eyes met. I had never once seen Danielle cry, yet here she was weeping as she proclaimed through her tears that she couldn't believe she had lived her entire life not knowing God existed. She had an experience beyond comprehension in Sedona, and realized that God was within her. She rushed over to me as quickly as possible and held me, blissfully rejoicing in her discovery. How I wished I could get to Sedona someday! I had no idea why I had even mentioned this place to her, since I had never been there. It must have been divine intervention and we both couldn't have been more grateful.

Looking up at her in this moment, I couldn't help but see a totally different being looking back at me. Her eyes were glowing and her breathtakingly beautiful violet aura filled the entire room. The atrophy and breakdown in her upper body were completely unnoticeable; she was glowing.

The look of surprise on her face when I opened my arms and asked her for a hug made me giggle; she couldn't believe she could actually touch me. Mom and I recounted the events of the last couple of weeks and she was astonished. Diazepam? Really? After all this miserable time, after all these countless doctors, Diazepam had relieved the contractions and spasms? Mom's exaggerated eye roll made me laugh as she recalled what Dr. Marten had said: that this was all in my head, I had been causing myself all this suffering due to anxiety, and the fact that Diazepam was having any effect was proof.

This made me pick up the information pamphlet that came with the medication from the pharmacy. There in black and white it said, "Diazepam, a medication used in the treatment of muscle spasms." I couldn't help but laugh hysterically as I highlighted the pertinent information and asked Mom to address an envelope to the attention of Dr. Marten. Mom quickly got up, asked Danielle to stay with me for a while and was out the door before she could even answer. I knew exactly where she was headed. She was personally hand-delivering that information pamphlet to Dr. Marten.

I couldn't have been more grateful for the opportunity to be alone with Danielle, I had so much to talk to her about. "Danielle I'm dying. We all know that. My organs are failing, making my skin green. I haven't eaten solid food in years, and my body is shutting down. Mom's denial has been shattered by everything she's witnessed in the past couple of weeks and she needs you. She won't talk to me about any of this because she thinks she has to remain strong, determined and positive. She's so scared. I know she has Sherrill to confide in and to be vulnerable with, and Sherrill couldn't be a more loving friend to both of us. I know that Sherrill will be here to help Mom after I'm gone, but you must promise me that you will take care of her.

"Promise me, Danielle, that you will stay with Mom and help her through this. Promise me that you will remind her constantly of what I want for her, and that is for her to live her life to the fullest. Tell her that being happy, spending time with my brothers, their families, her grandchildren, her siblings, and going on amazing adventures is the only way to keep my memory alive. Remind her that she hasn't lost me at all; that I am with her always. Promise me, Danielle, that you won't let her shut down or shut anyone out."

Danielle assured me that she would keep her promise and would do everything possible to help Mom through this. I then told her there wasn't much time left and that we should say what we needed to say to each other now, which we did. I loved her so deeply and was so grateful that she would be with Mom. The reassurance and the relief she gave me that day I could never put into words.

My friend Dina popped in to paint my toenails, knowing how utterly happy pretty toes made me. She owned her own spa and had been coming to the house every so often to cheer me up. Today was no different. My green skin, listless eyes, the drooping of the left side of my face as drool dripped out of the side of my mouth, and my fading form caught her off guard. She desperately tried to hide her reaction. I told her not to bother with the pretty toes, that I was just fine, and she knew exactly what I meant. Holding me as tightly as she could, I could feel the wetness of her tears against my cheek. This was our goodbye; Dina knew she would never see me again. I hoped she truly knew what she meant to me.

Over the next couple of days, I could feel my life force fading even more, and I knew the time was soon approaching. I hoped my brothers knew how much I loved them, and that they'd always been my heroes. I wished in that moment that I could hold them one last time. We had grown so far apart that I didn't want to see them or to let them see me like this. We had wasted so much time because of our beliefs, opinions, judgments and stupidity. I knew my brothers and their families would be here with Mom once this was all over, and that they would do everything they could for her. That was enough. That was all I needed. They didn't need to see me like this and would hopefully remember me as I was—the little girl with the biggest heart looking up to her big brothers... as I still did.

Sherrill stopped in a couple of days later, and although she didn't say anything, I knew she could no longer stand by and watch me die. As I held her closely, I knew this was the last time I would see her. I tearfully told her how much I loved and appreciated her, that I had cherished my time with her dog Zoe, and that it had absolutely extended my life. She had given me the greatest gift— the unconditional love of a dog who would lie beside me in bed all day long—after I lost Judge, then Titus. She lovingly expressed her feelings about how much she loved me, and quickly slipped out the door.

This was Sherrill, another very strong woman. No wonder she and Mom got along so well; they were both fierce. No wonder we all adored each other; we were all cut from the same cloth. I thought of all the women who had so selflessly surrounded me over the last few years and couldn't help but smile. What a fierce group of powerful women; all made of pure love. In that moment, the refection of the woman I had become was overwhelming, to say the least, when I considered the frightened girl filled with self-loathing who had begun this journey.

Kate still came to check up on me, although there wasn't much more she could do. There wasn't anything anyone could do. Seeing the helplessness in her eyes, I soon cancelled home care and all of their services. They were no longer necessary. Dr. L had been by to give me epidurals and spend some time with me, but he also knew there wasn't any more to be done. As he was leaving, we both took an extra long look at each other. No words were necessary.

Mom was at my side constantly and I could often feel her hand on my chest, checking for a heartbeat. I could hear her cry into her pillow at night, and I wanted more than anything to take her pain away. She had confided in Sherrill that every time she went out, she fully expected to find me dead upon her return. So she dreaded being away. The only time she ever left was to pick up medications or to run an errand that couldn't be postponed. She also worried every time she went to sleep; hence the hand on my chest every morning. I knew that hand, every inch of it.

Mom and I spent all of our time together, not losing one second, but I knew that morning that this was the day. I had zero appetite, which wasn't unusual, but not wanting to drink water for the last few days, now this was the telltale sign that my body was shutting down. I had to tell her. My heart wrenched at the thought, but she had to know. The life force within me was gone; I could feel myself slipping away and knew I wouldn't last the day. As I tearfully told her that I couldn't hold on any longer, she broke. She held me so tight, as if she could stop this from happening if she could just keep me wrapped in her arms and never let me go.

She tried to stay strong, as did I, but there was no strength left in either of us. How was I going to leave her? How was I ever going to leave her? Yes, she was Mom. Yes, she was my caregiver. Yes, she was my roommate. But she was so much more than that. She was my best friend and had been since the day I was born. I realized in that moment that I was part of her and she was part of me. We were one and could never be separated, not even by death.

She asked if there was anything I wanted; if I had one last wish, and there was. I wanted to dance one last time. She lifted my frail body out of bed, took me in her arms and the song "Thank You" by Johnny Reid[6] played on Country Music Television as we danced. We danced, held each other, and sobbed. This was our goodbye, and the words to this song said everything; exactly what I wanted to say to my mom:

"If I only had two words left to say to you,
With my last breath
I'd confess the truth to you.
You've never left my side even when I fell behind.
Thank you, thank you for the life you've given me.
Thank you for sharing all your love and all your dreams.
Thank you for every tear of happiness I've cried.
Thank you for laying down beside me here tonight."

Many realizations came upon me that day, as well as a sense of peace that surpassed all understanding. There was no mistaking this feeling; God was near. I grabbed a piece of a paper and a pen and began to write in my diary:

Don't miss the magic. Don't take one single moment for granted. All the ridiculousness I worried or argued about vanished instantly and weren't even part of my awareness. I was seeing with new eyes and a new heart. It is always said that every moment is a gift... but unfortunately this isn't realized until that moment is nearing your last. Promise me you'll hold your loved ones near, and never miss a chance to say "I love you." Promise me you'll see with eyes of love, a true love without condition or expectation. Promise me that my journey will make you see. The ego can ruin this for you; it can make you blind, judgmental and resentful, but you can stop this by recognizing the ego in yourself, as well as in others. You can choose to look through the ego and see the divine being that is you and the other. Don't let your eyes deceive you into believing we are separate... we are one!

If you found out you were dying and the doctor said you had thirty days to live, what would you do? Would you be kinder?

Love yourself more? Love freely with no fear? Be more patient? Try something new? Do you have any dreams that have been put on the back burner? Would you live them? Would you constantly worry about money and ruin your precious little time? Would you forgive and yearn to hold that person again? How about your partner, your love? Would you put your pride aside and ask for forgiveness? Children, grandchildren? Mom, Dad, friends?

WELL, YOU ARE RUNNING OUT OF TIME! We all are! It goes by in a millisecond, TRUST ME! Tomorrow does not exist; it is not promised to you! YOU, yes YOU, the one reading this... ARE DYING! What do YOU need to do? What do YOU need to complete? The journey that ALL OF US are on is the journey from Love to Love; what happens in between is YOUR CHOICE! *(End of diary entry.)*

As I read these words I hoped that someone would find them and publish them some day. I hoped that everything I had written would be published one day. I hoped that every single person would hear these words, truly hear these words, and realize this much earlier than I had. This realization did not have to wait until one was at the end of their life and actually facing death. My journey had not been for nothing, and my calling hadn't changed. If this reached even one person, then I had completed my mission.

It had been my main priority to ensure that Mom was taken care of financially, yet this hadn't even entered my awareness for the longest time. I was grateful that she would have the ability to live fully without limitation, but the only thing I cared about was loving her right here and right now. Everything else was irrelevant.

The little, insignificant resentments that had created such division within my family vanished without even a trace, leaving only unconditional love. There was nothing to forgive or to be forgiven for. There was just love. The thought of the precious time I had thrown away by being upset or angry was something I couldn't compute, and how I longed to have that time back now. The fear we perpetuate; the limitations we perceive; the beliefs we allow to separate us; the opinions we hold on to; the wasted time we spend worrying... all of these things are completely irrelevant. It is all an illusion, a smokescreen. As is death. I have always existed and will always exist.

In that moment, I knew all of this without a shadow of a doubt. I knew that God wasn't some man with a big beard in the sky looking down at us. He was pure love. Love beyond anything we can fathom. And this love is within each and every one of us. In that moment, I could feel it and I had become it.

PART TWO - HEAVEN CALLS

CHAPTER ELEVEN
Rebirth

Mom rushed through the door with nurses not far behind her. I had absolutely no idea what was going on, but I could see in Mom's face a glimmer of hope. She had been to a place called NutriChem™[7] and had spoken to a man by the name of Kent MacLeod. I couldn't help but wonder what in God's name she had been up to, but her renewed energy was palpable. Whatever it was, I didn't care; it was making her happy. The nurses drew all kinds of blood, Mom put all the vials, along with a urine sample, in a Styrofoam box, and off she went. I thought, "Yeah right, Mom. Good try, but we both know that nothing can be done. I mean, come on..."

The next thing I remember was hearing Kent's powerful voice on the other end of the line telling me to keep doing whatever I was doing—to fight and to give him 24 hours. Although I didn't understand a word he was saying or the scientific terms he was using, the tone of his voice was weirdly reassuring. He had tested over sixty levels in my blood and urine and had my results. He knew exactly what he needed to do. I'll never forget him saying, "I will try, Tina. I will try with everything I've got to help you. Hold on and keep fighting."

Just shy of two years being in and out of hospitals, with countless doctors and specialists saying to focus on quality of life with symptom relief, not on quantity of life... and this guy was going to save my life? Actually, saving my life was not possible; there was no life to save at this point. So he was going to bring me back to life?

Speaking with Dr. L shortly thereafter just confirmed my skepticism. He stated that we were looking for a "lucrative answer to death" since the NutriChem™ testing wasn't covered by Ontario Health Insurance Plan (OHIP) and would be an out-of-pocket expense. Mom was not having it whatsoever and lost her shit. She was beyond pissed. "What the hell do we fucking care about money at this point? And if there is even the slightest hope, what do we have to lose?" she yelled into the phone. Mom was one fierce lady, and not someone you wanted to piss off.

Witnessing her outburst, along with her renewed sense of hope, I couldn't help but fight with everything in me to hold on. I promised I wouldn't let go, not even for an instant, knowing full well that's all it would take. Kent spent 27 straight hours in his lab with his team, and he showed Mom exactly what to do with all these powders, capsules and creams. I was drinking so much juice that Mom had to empty the bed pan every time she turned around, but judging by the smile on her face, she didn't mind one bit.

She would carefully put the various powders into glasses, add the juice, mix it up, then bring it over with a long bendy straw so it would reach my mouth. Drinking lying down takes some skill, but after all this time I had become a pro. She would then put tons of capsules into my mouth followed by water to swallow them. As I watched her attentively read the instructions on the bottles, I couldn't help but fall madly in love with her all over again. She would rub the bio-identical hormone creams on my inner thighs and inner arms, taking her sweet time to ensure that it was all absorbed. The pain gel Kent had compounded was to be applied to my lower back and right hip, but the skin had to be clean prior to every application. Mom brought over a basin of warm water, the softest facecloth she could find, and a bar of soap. She would wash my entire lower back and right hip ever so gently, and three times a day, she would rub this pain gel into those areas until they were dry, while wearing a rubber glove.

We were constantly catching each other staring at one another, but neither of us would utter a word about what was happening...

or about the fact that I was still alive. This was just too good to be true. On the third day, my skin began to look like skin again, and we could actually see areas that were no longer green. There was something happening within me as well. This force I had so often spoken of, this life force, was returning, and I could feel energy reinvigorating my body. By the fifth day, Mom stared in disbelief as she saw the remote for the hospital bed in my hand and my head raised just enough to see the television. I was watching television again, and too immersed in the visuals to even acknowledge her reaction. But I certainly did notice. Still, we didn't utter a word until the morning she announced that she was heading out to look for a new car.

I had wanted a Nissan Rogue so badly that I couldn't help but feel huge excitement as she rushed out the door after filling me with the magical juice concoctions and putting the bed pan under me.

Beep, beep! Beep, beep! Beep, beep, beep! I could hear coming from the driveway as Mom ran into the house excited like a little girl on Christmas morning. I couldn't help but giggle. As she emptied the bed pan, she announced that she had found the car of my dreams and just knew I would freak. Feeling her excitement, I grabbed hold of the walker, and with her assistance, I actually got out of bed and made my way to the door. I had to see what she had found.

As I looked at the absolute dorkiest car I had ever seen, I was instantly madly in love and just had to take it for a test drive. The young handsome salesman named Curtis was a little surprised as he watched me make my way out to the vehicle with my walker. I was in my nightgown, but I didn't care in the very least. I hadn't driven in two years, and couldn't wait to punch that accelerator pedal and see what this baby could do. And that's exactly what I did, with Curtis in the passenger seat holding tightly onto the handle on the ceiling.

Pulling back into the driveway like Mario Andretti, I announced that the car was sold and asked how quickly we could have it.

After going through its endless options and choosing which ones we wanted (which just had to include the mood lights on the floor and the shag rug on the dash), the papers were signed and the car was paid in full. We had to wait for the requested options and the rust protection, but due to what Curtis had been a part of on the day of the test drive, the Nissan "Cube" was in our driveway within the week.

Mom and I were so happy. We finally admitted that I was going to be just fine, as we fell into each other's arms and sobbed. We just couldn't believe that I was still here and that I was actually sitting, standing, walking and even using the commode beside my bed—I no longer needed the bed pan. Mom slowly helped me up the stairs, got in the shower with me to hold me up, and cried as she witnessed what she hadn't seen in years. Her daughter was actually taking a shower, lathering glorious smelling soaps onto her body, and washing her long black hair. Tears rolled down her face in sheer gratitude for this experience, and she screamed for joy. The smells, the sensations, the water, the cleanliness, were too much to bear as I fell into Mom's arms sobbing. I was here. I was really here. I was alive to live this moment, and to share it with her. I was really going to be okay.

The huge fluffy warm towels wrapped around my head and body cocooned me as I climbed into Mom's recliner so she could wash my sheets after all this time. She gathered everything into her arms and I noticed the unmistakable sound of the bed pan as she threw it on top of the pile with the biggest smile on her face. It made me giggle like a schoolgirl. Our washer and dryer were downstairs, and she was bringing it downstairs with her to put it away. It was really over; I was no longer bedridden.

Mom and I had one thing left to do. We were soon in the car and on our way. Dressed in real clothes and not in a hospital gown for the first time in almost two years, I climbed the five or six steps and knocked on the door while Mom stood by the car with the biggest grin on her face. When he answered the door, I'm sure Dr. L thought I was an apparition. His eyes popped out of his head as the oh-so familiar sound "boing" flashed across my mind making me giggle loudly. I was soon hugging him, announcing that it was me. It was really me, and I was just fine.

He held me at arm's length, carefully inspecting me from head to toe with great scrutiny, not believing his eyes. "I'm really here, Dr. L! It's really me!" Mom laughed with such heart, it felt like mine was going to burst. Dr. L soon wanted every detail about this place called NutriChem[8] and wanted to know exactly what this man named Kent MacLeod had done. This didn't surprise me in the slightest.

This state cannot be explained nor understood unless personally experienced. There just are no words to convey what coming back to life feels like. I truly believed that I had it all prior to the accident, but I realized as I was living out my last moments, that I had it all… *wrong*. After the accident, all sense of identity had been brutally removed but quickly replaced with "victim." Eventually, this proved to be intolerable. This is suffering and pain's sole purpose for existing.

Labeling or defining something does not mean we grasp its meaning, even in the slightest. Everything in existence is unknowable, unfathomable and a miracle waiting to be discovered, once all assumptions have been dropped. When this happens, the magic witnessed and so easily accepted as a child returns, along with an awe-inspiring innocence, trust and joie de vivre.

Everything was shiny and new again as it had been when I was a child. Touching the tree in our back yard, listening to Mom tell one of her stories, or even just watching my toes wiggle made me weep with such overwhelming glee, awe and love. The energies and auras in nature and around people had returned, flooding my mind with memories of the magic I had always seen while growing up. "Mini-fireflies" happily danced all around me, and I witnessed everything with new eyes.

Time no longer existed. I had absolutely zero perception of time. Fascination was my state of being, regardless of my surroundings.

Here I was in our townhouse that we'd lived in for years... yet nothing was familiar. It was as if I had never been here before. The wicker end tables on each side of my bed seemed brighter as I curiously brushed the wicker with my fingers, feeling the aliveness within them. And brightest of all was Mom. As I lay there looking at her, I wondered if I had ever truly seen her before. The curvature of her nose, the eyelashes peaking ever so beautifully above her eyes, and the deep chestnut color of her eyes sparkling as they looked back at me. The astonishing sense of love within me brought tears to my eyes; I just couldn't fathom this kind of love. I wasn't feeling love, I had become love.

Everywhere I went, people were drawn to me without having any idea as to why. Mom would stand back and watch as complete strangers approached me for whatever reason, and would start telling me their whole life stories. I attentively listened while filled with so much love, so much awe. I took the person in my arms and held them as I whispered, "I love you; you are so beautiful." All I saw was love, everywhere. Attitudes and behaviors were completely irrelevant, as all I could see was the very essence of every being lighting up and surrounding them entirely. This beauty, this absolutely breathtaking beauty, was in everyone and everything.

Every morning was a gift waiting to be ripped open as my consciousness returned. As I heard the sounds of the coffee maker and the smell permeated the room, a smile crept over my face and my eyes flickered open in anticipation of this moment. I was still here, spellbound by the breath tickling my nose. I stretched my body in gratitude for every sensation. Like a little girl on Christmas morning, I couldn't wait to discover what gifts were awaiting me. I was still here.

Music had played a major role in my journey, but I fully admit that I hadn't truly heard it before. Each instrument was magnified in detail as the melody filled my entire being. Mom watched adoringly, which I know led to this next adventure. She was bringing me to an Aaron Pritchett concert in a town nearby. Arrangements had been made for my wheelchair and I wasn't embarrassed at all to be seen in it. I excitedly anticipated being part of such a miraculous experience. Yes, it was absolutely a miraculous experience; I was still here.

We played the tunes in the car full blast all the way to the small town Aaron was playing in, singing and swaying our bodies and giggling all the way. When we arrived at the gate we met Roxanne. What a beautiful woman. She and her husband Ron radioed ahead as she told us to just keep going until we reached the bleachers. I was a little confused because there were gates everywhere. As we approached each gate, there was someone there to open it, and we eventually parked right at the bleachers themselves.

Before I knew it, there was a man at Mom's door. She pointed to me and he went around the Cube, opened the back door and took out my wheelchair. He had assumed Mom was the one who required the wheelchair since I looked young, radiant and very physically capable. I had to giggle. He then grabbed me as if I was a tiny little girl, lifted me out of the car and carefully placed me into the wheelchair. He pushed me all the way to the front of the bleachers.

As I sat there looking at all the people, I was spellbound by the auras excitedly dancing around them in every color in existence. It made me gasp; it literally took my breath away. The man who had so effortlessly lifted me into his arms was now sitting beside me, and he passed me his cellphone and a bottle of water. His name was Ernie and he explained that he was leaving his cell phone with me. All I had to do was press this button and he would be at my beck and call all night to take me to the bathroom, bring me water or whatever Mom and I needed. Without waiting for a reply, he was gone in his little red buggy.

Due to the amount of water I drank, I kept Ernie very busy that night, but he didn't mind in the least. He would pull up in the little red car, lift me into his arms and gently put me in the passenger seat. We would drive to the portables laughing all the way. Then he would take me into his arms once again, bring me into the washroom, and leave me as he closed the door, being the perfect gentleman.

We had an opportunity to talk as he was giving me a tour of the grounds and he couldn't help but ask what had happened to me. I told him the whole story and how blessed I was to be here; that just five weeks ago I had lived out my last days. He was astonished and couldn't believe that the radiant girl he was looking at was ever sick. He told me I was beautiful beyond words and that he couldn't believe I was still single. This was a recurrent theme all night, and I giggled at his insistence. I told him about my first love, Kevin, but that he had moved on long ago... and that I loved being alone and would be for the rest of my life. This was beyond Ernie's comprehension.

Sitting back in the wheelchair thoroughly enjoying the concert, savoring every moment, I couldn't help but be in awe of the treatment I had received. Tears of pure love streamed down my face. This was love. My moment was interrupted by the movement of my chair as I was being pushed through the crowd. I was panic-stricken as I sensed Mom getting further and further away from me. I turned to see that it was Ernie pushing me, but I had no idea what was happening as we bumped into every person in our way.

A girl named Linda soon took over and Ernie cleared the people before me, and I heard over the speaker, "Let her through." Security was now surrounding us, clearing a straight path to the stage. I was lifted out of the chair, and I watched the chair being lifted onto the stage. I repeatedly yelled, "My legs don't work!" scared I would be dropped. I was soon on stage with Aaron Pritchett and his band! What an experience, and holy loud! I giggled as I watched the drummer hit the beats with the biggest grin on his face as he looked at me.

I couldn't believe that I was actually here to live this. After the last few songs, I was wheeled off stage down a side ramp where Aaron himself soon came to meet me. What an absolute sweetheart. I then met the entire band and they handed me all kinds of autographed pictures saying, "Loved rawking with you, Tina." [rocking]

This had been the most exhilarating experience of my entire life, and as we arrived at the motel, neither Mom nor I could stop smiling. I was deaf for days, but I loved every minute of it. Never had I been made to feel so special, and it occurred to me that my perception of myself had completely changed. This wheelchair had nothing to do with who I was, and never had. My physical form did not define me in any way, nor did it have anything to do with the essence of who I was. This was reflected back to me that night in everyone around me, especially Ernie. I would treasure this man always for everything he had done and everything he was. His words I will cherish forever as he saw through my physical form to the being of pure love that I was in his arms. He told me that I would make some very deserving man extremely happy one day, as his wife had made him, and that I deserved to be madly loved and adored. His words filled me with such bliss and bewilderment, and although I was determined to be single for the rest of my life, I must admit it sparked something within me. I couldn't help but think of Kevin.

Then the day came when I finally had the privilege of meeting Kent MacLeod, the man who had singlehandedly brought me back to life. Here is part of the letter I gave to Kent. It is dated October 1, 2009:

> Because of NutriChem™⁹ I feel better today than I have in thirteen years. This is not only due to the pain management, but also the physical, mental and emotional improvements. I have energy to get to know my family again, to make new friends, to go out and have fun; to actually start living life and make plans for the future. To dream again.
>
> I have been waiting a long time, and I had even given up, but I can finally purchase a house, which had previously been impossible, due to the extent of my physical, emotional and mental deterioration. From complete immobility, starvation, horrendous and unrelenting symptoms and organ failure, to walking, driving, being nourished and living—this is a miracle indeed.

There are no words to express how I feel about NutriChem™. You have saved my life, plain and simple, which countless doctors were unable to do. "Thank you" does not even come close to expressing the immense gratitude I feel for you. How could it? What do you say to a person who has brought you back to life? You have given me my life back, a dream that had died many years ago.

There are still surgeries to get through, but you've given me the opportunity to even require them, and I know everything will be okay, since it already is. I would not change the last thirteen years even if I could, because it has made me the woman I am today. I am very proud of her. It has also made this moment that much sweeter.

I have recommended you to everyone I know and even people I don't know. Your pamphlets and cards are in my vehicle, just in case I run into someone who needs help. Witnessing such a miracle with his own eyes, my physician is also spreading the word. You have given him an actual tool to help his other patients. *(End of letter excerpt.)*

I was now face-to-face with Kent, and as tears streamed down my face, all I could do was hug him as I repeatedly mouthed the words, "Thank you." I was soon being embraced by various members of Kent's team, who were here to witness the miracle right before them. A miracle indeed, and nothing short of one.

I was then introduced to Dr. Buckley, the most brilliant, heart-centered woman I had ever met. She was fearlessly and courageously taking me on as her patient. Little did I know, she would keep me alive by closely monitoring me every four months and adjusting my levels accordingly. This care has given me the privilege of writing these words, finishing my book, as I sit here now.

There truly are no words but *family.* This was my family. As the years passed, I fell in love with my NutriChem™4 family even more so, as we now traveled this journey together. The unconditional love and support of Kent, Dr. Buckley, Yolanda, Laura, Grace, Lois and many others was beyond anything I could imagine, and still is to this day. Yes, this was my family and always would be.

Approximately two weeks following this love-filled day at NutriChem™⁵, I found out that Aaron was playing not far from where I lived in Ottawa. I couldn't wait to see him in concert again. My cousin Danielle and her sister Joelle joined me, as we slowly made our way to the stage, which was at the back of the grounds. Danielle had lost much of her upper body ability due to ALS, and I was using arm braces by this time, so Joelle had to carry all our stuff. We got there early so we could get a front seat. Upon arriving, I noticed the girl named Linda who had so courageously stepped up at the last concert to push my wheelchair through that massive crowd. I thanked her profusely for being such a fierce woman. We exchanged contact information and the concert soon began.

As I watched Aaron doing what he does best, I couldn't help but reminisce about being on stage with him and his band. This resulted in the biggest smile on my face as I sang along with every lyric all night long. After the concert ended, I brought Danielle and Joelle over to meet Aaron. He noticed that I was up on my feet, and he lovingly grabbed me to give me the biggest hug in celebration. I knew he would always have a special place in my heart, and as I hugged him back, I hoped he knew what his music and being on his stage meant to me.

We slowly made our way back to our vehicle. We had to take breaks repeatedly, and as I looked over at Joelle loaded down with all our stuff, Danielle and I broke into a laughing fit, and Joelle said, "You bunch of gimps!" in protest. These two girls always cracked me up. Their wit, their unapologetic honesty, and their absolute lack of sympathy was enlightening.

I had long ago realized the effect that pity had on me, and how it shattered my fighting spirit. During the last few years of home care and hospitals, Mom would unceremoniously remove anyone who looked at me with pity-filled eyes. She knew full well that they weren't seeing me at all. That's the reason Kate had been the last one standing. She poked fun at me and didn't have a pitiful bone in her body. This invigorated my spirit, brought some normalcy and made me giggle incessantly. If we couldn't laugh at this situation then what was the point?

Being so sick with a fading form and a dwindling life force, I certainly didn't need any lower vibrations around me. Pity was the most toxic energy in existence for me; anger or hate weren't even in the same ball park. It was draining, and it instigated self-pity, which is not a vibration someone dealing with an illness (never mind death) can handle. I loved the joyous laughter, the making fun and the blissful vibration Mom and Kate carried. They were uplifting, and another contributing factor to the fact that I was still here. If I had been surrounded by sympathy and pity, I would surely have been gone long ago. There were still many procedures and surgeries to go through to repair the spine and the hip, but I was different. With childlike curiosity, I had become the witness instead of the participant.

Linda and I had become good friends, and our mutual love of country music brought us many adventures, including the Burl's Creek concert. We were excitedly looking forward to it, although Mom couldn't help but worry. I called ahead to ensure they were set up for people with disabilities and was assured that they had made every arrangement. This brought some peace of mind for Mom, considering she wasn't going to be there. The day soon arrived for us to make the five-hour drive.

Upon arriving, we found a handicap-friendly parking space, but I noticed that the stage was an insane distance away. I remembered them telling me on the phone that they had golf carts to transport people with disabilities. We were right at the gate waiting for it to open, and while the crowd was amassing behind us, my legs could no longer support me. Linda helped by holding me up. The gates should have opened long ago, and the amount of people behind us was really worrying me.

A woman with beautiful power and spirit approached to speak with me. Her presence was palpable. Her name was Ivy Henriksen, and she was the Accessibility Advisor for that district. She was soon taking on Security stating the laws and demanding that the gates be temporarily opened to allow the people with disabilities to go on ahead. Otherwise, we would be trampled by the crowd. They weren't listening at all, threatening to have her removed from the property. But she wasn't backing down. What an experience to see such a warrior woman in action; I loved her instantly.

The gates suddenly opened. I was struck with fear, desperately attempting to get out of the way, but it wasn't possible. Linda and Ivy shielded my body from every bump, kick and shove until it was over. They then assisted me to the stage, which was a long way away. I was exhausted, and they never left my side. The warrior woman in Ivy revived my own warrior spirit that very night. I cherish her selfless act on behalf of a total stranger. She is an inspiration to me, and she became a very dear friend. Mom was none too pleased upon hearing what happened, but I told her that I was fine, and that I had thoroughly enjoyed myself. Besides, I had the privilege of meeting Ivy and seeing her in action.

Over the next couple of months I regained the ability to walk unassisted, but the right leg continued to falter every so often. This resulted in many falls, smashing my head, face and body to the ground. The nausea also continued, but I had become accustomed to this, and even to the vomiting. There was so much happiness to be enjoyed.

Mom finally retired—-what a joyous and proud day for me. No longer did she have to work ridiculous hours to support me; we could spend all of our precious time together. There was someone I desperately needed to see, so I excitedly jumped into the car and made my way to her spa. Dina, the one who had shared goodbyes with me not so long ago, soon caught sight of me walking towards her. In utter shock and disbelief, she began to cry. She could not grasp that it was me or how I was standing before her. I reached out my arms to take her into an embrace. "Yes, it's me Dina. It's really me." I filled her in on everything that had happened, and she reveled in each detail. I told her we were looking to buy a house, and Dina, who was a sharp business lady with many contacts, handed me a realtor's card. Soon I was meeting with Cammie. Providing her with my wish list, she went to work finding Mom and me our dream home.

I had lost track of the number of houses we had looked at, as we made our way to yet another one. As we passed by a new subdivision, a familiar energy washed over me, filling me with an abundance of excitement. I yelled enthusiastically for Cammie to stop and turn around; I wanted to see that big yellow house we had just passed. She made a U-turn and drove to the house. We parked in front of it, and I knew this was it. This was my house!

I skipped through the snow to the little plastic box to grab the listing. As I perused the information I already knew this was my house. Everyone said this house was much too large for just Mom and me, that it would require way too much effort to clean, and that I was dreaming in color... but I wouldn't back down. This energy, this place—this was the one. After touring the inside and meeting with Rosie, my senior banking officer and mortgage specialist, the papers were soon signed and we were moving in. We were so excited. Sitting in that house with Mom, I couldn't help but sob. I was here; I was able to live this moment with her.

For the next couple of weeks we shopped for all the furnishings. Since it was a large brand-new house, we had lots to furnish, but we loved every single second of it.

CHAPTER TWELVE

The Love of My Life

By April of 2010 the Internet was finally hooked up. I was playing on Facebook when I received a "suggested friend" from Nancy Blackwell. I couldn't breathe. My heart raced upon seeing his last name. It was the sister of Kevin, my Kevin. My first love, the one I had never stopped loving, the one who had given me the promise ring I still wore and had never taken off. Tears came to my eyes as I quickly sent the friend request, then waited in anticipation as I checked out his profile. Looking at his picture made my heart skip a beat. I still so deeply loved him! I noticed that his relationship status was single. Where was he? How was he? We had so much catching up to do after 25 years!

After a dream-filled night full of memories, I awoke in the morning to a message from him—from Kevin, the love of my life! I had changed; I wasn't the young, capable teenage girl he knew all those years ago. I was a grown woman who had disabilities and I was scared to death. Feelings I swore I would never again allow myself to feel came flooding back. I desperately tried to keep my cool. After a few messages, we exchanged phone numbers.

I saw the number on the telephone and picked up the receiver. Hearing his voice brought me right back to 1989. My Kevin! His voice hadn't changed in the slightest, and it pierced right through the armor I had worked so hard to build. But I wouldn't let him know that my heart was still his. I kept making excuses not to go see him, knowing exactly what would happen if I did.

Over the next three weeks we messaged and spoke daily and I played it cool. But he saw right through it. He sent me a message saying, "I know who you are, Tina. You can try to hide it all you want, but you aren't fooling me at all." He had me. I called to tell him that I was coming to see him; that I was catching a fight across the country in two days. I was scared shitless but I couldn't stand it one more second. I had to see him.

I was sitting in the plane high above the clouds, and memories of yesterday, of us, came flooding back as I played with his promise ring. I needed him to take this slowly and told him this. I had been alone for nine years and was completely resigned in remaining so. I was scared and unsure; we had to go slow. During my layover I could feel the anticipation building, as I would soon be with him. I sent him a text notifying him that I was boarding the last flight.

This journey had been so long; we hadn't been together in 25 years. It felt like an eternity, yet it felt like yesterday. This was all very surreal, considering I was dying just a few short months ago. Now I was about to see the love of my life again! I was in complete disbelief when the pilot announced that we were preparing for descent. I looked out the window watching as we got closer to the landing strip. My heart began to race as I tried to prepare myself for what was about to happen.

With my legs shaking beneath me, I made my way out of the tiny aircraft and into the airport where he was waiting, arms crossed, stiffly standing as if trying to hold himself up. Our eyes met. I walked over and right into his arms. Am I really here? Am I really in Kevin's arms? This feeling that had so long eluded me—this feeling of *home* that I had yearned for, searched for—had not been about a house, an apartment or a building. It had been about Kevin all along. I was home. I was finally home.

We were shy as he clumsily opened the passenger door to his truck to allow me in, closing it behind me. As he made his way around to the driver's side, I couldn't help but stare in disbelief. It was really him; I was really with Kevin. This wasn't a dream, although it certainly felt like one. We made small talk on the 30-minute drive to his house. Neither of us really knew what to say, making the silent gaps very uncomfortable. Sitting in that truck, I wanted so badly to lift the console and slide over next to him, but I couldn't make myself move. I had told him in no uncertain terms to take it slowly, so he didn't know what to do.

Finally we arrived and I was meeting his two beautiful kids, Kathleen and Kody. As I watched them speak and move, I could see their dad's mannerisms and features, which made me fall in love with them instantly. The kids definitely broke the ice, but the awkwardness I was feeling wasn't dissipating in the least. I was trying to control my feelings and take this slowly, but it wasn't working. I was more than thankful when the evening came to an end so I could sleep this off.

Kevin showed me the bedroom, then grabbed a pillow and a blanket, heading to the couch, when I blurted out, "We are both adults Kevin. We can certainly share the same bed and keep our hands to ourselves. You're not sleeping on the couch." We clumsily readied ourselves for bed , not saying a word as we climbed into our respective sides, just like we did as teenagers—which made me giggle as we drifted off to dreamland.

I woke up not knowing where I was, as the surroundings were completely unfamiliar... until I turned around and saw Kevin. I quietly laid back down. Facing him, I studied every inch of his face, still not believing I was really there. He hadn't changed a bit and neither had my feelings for him. The familiar shape of his face, the jagged edge of his jaw, the perkiness of his lips, which I remembered on mine like it was yesterday. I knew those lips. I couldn't understand how I loved this man so much, though we had been apart for 25 years.

I made my way out of the bedroom, sat on the couch and sent Mom a message to tell her how I felt. Tears rolled down my face and onto my phone. I was alive. I was alive to live this moment and I still couldn't believe it. I was in love with Kevin, always had been, and here I was with a second chance. After everything

I'd gone through, including living out my last days, how was this even possible? Mom was deliriously happy upon reading my message; she had also always loved Kevin. Because she knew full well what my plans had been up until this point, she was hoping this would change everything.

After realizing I was going to live, I prepared a new Last Will and Testament. Mom found it while we were organizing our new house, and it devastated her to read it. I had written that a life without Mom wasn't a life at all, and that I had no one to share mine with. I wasn't married, I was vehemently opposed to ever letting anyone into my life again, and I had lost the ability to have children. So I had made the decision that I was going to be with Mom, come what may.

I had written exactly what was to be done with my estate, as well as a letter to my big brothers. They were not to weep or be sad for I was with Mom, where I belonged, and I was happy. Everything was to be divided amongst their children. I wrote that I loved them beyond anything they could imagine and always had. Mom and I had a long tearful conversation but there was no changing my mind. I was not going to hire someone to take care of me so I could live a life of solitude and she knew it. Although we never spoke of it again, I knew it was weighing heavily on her mind and she was hoping beyond hope that I would let Kevin into my heart.

I planned a surprise birthday party for Kevin at a restaurant. It was early afternoon and everything was set. As I sat across from him at his kitchen table, I couldn't stand it one more second. I walked around the table, sat in his lap and wrapped my arms around him. The moment we embraced took my breath away, literally. We held each other tightly for what seemed like an eternity, neither of us letting go until I was finally able to catch my breath. I turned my face to meet his, to kiss those oh-so-familiar lips. I knew those lips.

This was my first love, the love of my life, and I loved him more than I ever thought possible. My heart was still his after all these years, and being in his arms, kissing him, was beyond surreal. I was indeed home. That night at the restaurant with his kids, his sister Nancy and her husband Joe, and their now grown children, I savored every moment, realizing the blessing of celebrating his birthday—although it still felt like a dream. We talked, cried and held each other all night, catching up on everything we had missed in each other's lives. We were falling even more in love.

The days went by too quickly and it was soon time to go back to Ottawa. It cut me to the core. The window of the tiny plane was covered in steam as I sobbed uncontrollably. The fight attendant asked if I was okay as she handed me a tissue. I quickly wiped the window, apologizing. Then I caught sight of Kevin's truck parked along the highway waiting to watch my plane take off, and I lost it even more. I wanted to get off that plane and run back to him as fast as I could. As I pointed to the truck, I told the girl sitting beside me that there was the love of my life and I was leaving him again.

I realized at that moment that I couldn't imagine my life without him, and that I loved him beyond words. I soon heard the words, "Go to him sweetie, get off the plane and go to him!" in a masculine voice coming from somewhere behind me. But I couldn't; I had too many responsibilities. I had just bought a house, and Danielle was living with us and needed help. I had to go back. As the plane took off, I watched Kevin get further and further away until he was out of sight and I cried myself to sleep.

Our house didn't even remotely resemble the house I had left twelve short days ago. It brought about a sense of vastness due to its size. Once in his arms again, I knew instantly that home was Kevin. He always had been and always would be. But the situation seemed impossible. He lived on the other side of the country and had children. I couldn't even consider leaving my area due to the medical team with which I was blessed. We were in quite the predicament.

Obviously, taking it slow was out of the question once we saw each other; 25 years apart will do that. We had picked up right where we left off, as if no time had passed. But these doubts and fears about our situation persisted. We messaged each other many times every day and called just to hear each other's voices.

Mom and I were soon leaving for a trip up north. I couldn't wait to get out of this huge, empty house and perhaps clear some of these thoughts of the impossibility of the future of our relationship. A road trip with Mom was just what the doctor ordered. We hit the highway with the tunes blasting as we sang along.

It was a hometown reunion we were attending, but there was someone missing... Kevin. Kevin and I grew up in the same little town and knew each other's families for most of our lives, yet he wasn't there. Mom and I visited his dad, his sister, Tina, and on our way home, we stopped in to spend some time with his mom. This brought back all the feelings I had for each one of them. I loved Kevin's family immensely and had always considered them my family. Memories of Joyce flooded my mind. She had been such a fierce big sister when I was living with Kevin as a teenager; and had taken me under her wing. I wondered how she was doing and couldn't wait to give her the biggest hug. How I had missed them. Everywhere I went, Kevin's absence was magnified, making me miss him even more.

Upon arriving home, the personalized ringtone for Kevin rang on my phone. I picked it up quickly to see that it was a text message and couldn't wait to see what he had written. There were no words, just a link to a song called "This I Promise You" by NSYNC[10]. I went out to the garage where I could listen without interruption. I clicked the link and began to sob when I heard the words. I was still his:

I've loved you forever,
In lifetimes before
And I promise you never...
Will you hurt anymore
I give you my word
I give you my heart (give you my heart)
This is a battle we've won
And with this vow,
Forever has now begun...

Mom appeared in the garage and saw me crying. She asked what was wrong but I couldn't speak. She sat beside me, took me into her arms, and held me tightly until I was able to finally gather myself enough to tell her what had been weighing so heavily on my mind... and had been since I left him. "Mom, this is impossible. He lives in Alberta with his kids and I can't leave here. We just bought a house, Danielle is living with us, and I can't leave my doctors. This is never going to work. I'm just prolonging the inevitable and causing both of us more pain by going out to see him again. I can't believe this, Mom. We get a second chance but it's not a chance at all."

Mom wiped my tears and I will never forget her words to me that day: "This isn't the woman I raised. My fearless daughter knows that if she wants something bad enough, she will find a way. She won't let anything stop her. You and Kevin have loved each other forever with a love so pure, so unconditional, that it has stood the test of time. What you and Kevin have is rare. This kind of love happens once... and that's if you're lucky. Are you going to waste this second chance? That's not the girl I raised. You've been given a second chance, my beautiful girl, and it's up to you what you do with it. Don't you dare let me, Danielle, this house, the kids or anything stand in the way of what you two share. Get on a plane and go get the love of your life. There's nothing stopping you."

Of course this was exactly what I needed to hear; Mom had a knack for that. I was on a plane the next day to be with Kevin. Three weeks later, he was on a plane to Ontario with me to build two bedrooms, a den and a bathroom in the basement for the kids. I looked out at the clouds below us the entire trip, and I couldn't believe this was really happening. We would actually be sharing our lives together and planning our future. I wasn't dreaming; this was real. I was here to live this moment.

With immense gratitude and love, I thanked God for such a beautiful life. It had all been a gift, for I wasn't even expected to be alive by now! If anything had been different, if even one little thing was pulled from the equation, it would have changed everything.

Danielle soon bought a house with her parents and moved back to London, Ontario. How I missed her! But I knew she was exactly where she needed to be. Kevin and I were so excited as we mapped out the floor plan with masking tape, discussing room sizes and color schemes for the kids. We could barely contain our excitement. The build took approximately two months and we loved every second of being together. We couldn't wait for the kids to see their new rooms. Kathleen was going to stay with her mom and visit during the summer break, and Kody was coming to live with us, visiting his mom every chance he got. Everything was ready. It was time to fly back to Alberta, pack up and make the five-day drive back to Ontario with Kody.

Our first Christmas was beyond anything I could imagine, and no words can express the range of emotions I felt. Since it had been just Mom and I for ten years, we didn't have any decorations or even a tree. Mom spent Christmas Day with my brother and his family, but the rest of the holiday we just relaxed together and watched movies. Being a huge fan of Christmas and presents, Kevin insisted we buy a tree and decorate. This was foreign to me, so he and Kody took care of everything. Sitting in my usual place on the couch looking at the tree, the presents, and the beautifully decorated table with four place settings, tears filled my eyes with overwhelming bliss and joy. I realized that I had a family to share my life with; I had a family to celebrate Christmas with; I had a legacy.

I was still unable to sit at the kitchen table, but that sure didn't diminish the gratitude I felt for this miraculous blessing. Never in a million years could I have imagined that this could happen. I knew that if it hadn't been Kevin, it wouldn't have been anyone. I loved him to the very core of my being; I always had. And I cherished every moment we were together. I loved Kody and Kathleen's mom, Kim, for bringing these two beautiful children into my life. I couldn't have been more grateful to her.

I walked over to the filing cabinet in the office, reached into a file and removed My Last Will and Testament. As I tearfully read what my wishes had been, I couldn't believe how everything had so completely changed—in the blink of an eye it seemed. While I was putting each page of the Will into the shredder, I noticed a colorful piece of paper that had fallen out of the file. I couldn't believe my eyes when I saw what it was! It was the DVD insert with the image of the genie from The Secret, which I had removed from the case and written my biggest dreams on all those years ago. I had completely forgotten about this, yet here it was. And every single dream listed had come true except two:

- Love of my life (Kevin) ***
- Claim settled (I included the amount and it was to the dollar) ***
- Beautiful brand new house on the outskirts of Ottawa ***
- Living on a lake with lots of land (This is what Kevin and I had dreamed of since we were kids, and we were in the process of making this dream come true.)
- Mom retired ***
- An awesome fuel-efficient car that is bought and paid for ***
- Financially independent; debt-free with money in the bank ***
- A life filled with love, joy, gratitude and laughter ***
- Using my life in service ***
- Perfect health (This was still my biggest dream.)

I had planted these seeds, written them down, and regardless of the doubts, obstacles and challenges that inevitably follow any dream, I had stayed the course to reach the celebration of manifestation. Seeing it all there in black and white, I couldn't help but realize how truly blessed I was. Dreams really do come true if you believe. If you choose to use your emotions as they were intended, they are the most accurate navigation system in existence. A negative emotion is a signpost indicating that what you're thinking is not true, so you can bring awareness to your thoughts and get back on course. Use your emotional navigation system to follow your joy, listen to your heart, and use your imagination to feel the achievements of your dreams as if they have already happened.

It wasn't lost on me how badly I wanted what I had right now. I had visualized countless times in vivid detail what this all would feel like. There was no comparison. This was beyond words. And I knew the manifestation of the last three dreams on my list was just a matter of time. The Law of Attraction was certain and I had truly learned years ago to no longer manifest "by default." I stayed focused on my preferred state of being while dropping the rest.

The constant road trips were painful, but due to my definition of "Physically Accelerated In Non-resistance" (PAIN), we actually enjoyed ourselves. Dr. B had stated over and over that I did not have MS, and that we should further investigate the annular tear at L5-S1, the disc protrusion, and the bone cysts in the right hip. The procedure I underwent at a hospital two hours from our house brought us closer to the answer. The doctor carefully pushed a long needle into the S1 joint, filling it with an analgesic. I could hear the needle crunching through the bones on its way to the target, which made me quiver, but it really wasn't that painful. The procedure resulted in absolutely no feeling in my right leg.

When I arrived home, Kevin was waiting for the car, ready to carry me into our home. When he lifted me into his arms, I fell even more in love with him. He stayed in bed with me day in and day out, not leaving my side for anything other than to eat. I was still unable to eat solid food, so Mom would bring me my liquid shakes in bed, where she knew I had to be. This was normal for us. Although Kevin was completely unaware of the severity of my condition when I was in Alberta, he now fully understood. His faith never wavered however, and he was supporting, loving and encouraging me every step of the way.

I had another procedure done in Montreal, which concurrently proved that the annular tear at the L5-S1 disc was the cause of my symptoms. The specialist injected five needles, one into each nerve of the S1 joint, injecting each with laser precision, completely blocking any pain coming from the joint. My symptoms didn't change in the slightest, so the S1 joint was ruled out, leaving the annular tear as the culprit, which we had suspected all along.

With Dr. B's guidance, Dr. Buckley had finally gotten to the bottom of the issue, and I couldn't have been more relieved. The specialist in Montreal immediately put me on the list for a Discogram, followed by IDET (Intradiscal Electrothermal Therapy) surgery. Although the possible complications were rare, they were alarming. They could include bleeding, temporary numbness or weakness, spinal headache, nerve damage, hoarseness of voice and paralysis. I had completely healed my neck with meditation and didn't doubt in the least that I could do it again. I just had to use caution when walking, and ensure I had something to hold onto to prevent another injury from a fall. Kody had picked me up off the floor a few times, as had Kevin.

All of this had to be put on the back burner, however, as another surgery became more crucial. Due to the severe loss of blood I was experiencing every month, Dr. Buckley advised an emergency hysterectomy. We quickly met with the surgeon, who was knowledgeable, forthcoming and very funny as he explained his recommendations in detail. The surgery was scheduled immediately. So, two months after Kevin moved in, I had to go under anesthesia again. I knew the elevated risks in my case due to years of medications, procedures and surgeries, as well as the fragile state of my organs.

I was relieved that none of my doctors mentioned anything about these risks to Mom or Kevin. I could handle it, since I could witness my thoughts, opinions and beliefs, and choose the outcome I desired. I had long ago mastered the ability to keep my focus on my preference while completely ignoring any contradictory facts, opinions or data, realizing they had no basis in reality unless I believed them. Remaining in a state of remembrance using visualization instead of projecting into the future, I visualized the outcome of the hysterectomy as successful, without complications, and that I was now happily at home. This technique worked beautifully for maintaining my alignment and eliminating unnecessary and unhelpful lower vibrational thoughts and feelings. Mom and Kevin couldn't help but worry, and I understood. But I could handle this.

Letter to Kevin Dated September 1, 2010

My love, I believe with every fiber of my being that everything will be okay, but there's still a chance for complications and I don't want to leave things unsaid.

Kevin, if something does happen, please don't look at it like you've lost something, because you could never lose me. Remember that we were given the biggest gift, a second chance. These last few months have been the happiest, most fulfilling time of my life and I wouldn't change one thing. You make me so happy, babe, and I've loved you for as long as I can remember. I am so proud of the person you are and I love you. I always have and always will.

Of course it is natural to be sad when you lose someone you love, but I don't want you to spend the rest of your life being sad. I want you to be loved, and that may mean giving your heart to someone else. Sitting here as I write this, it's unthinkable, but if something does happen to me, promise me that you will love again, totally and completely. Kevin, you are the love of my life. I may have "lost" you for a while but I know that you can't really lose someone or ever be separated. I'll forever and always be with you, regardless of where life takes us, and the love we share will live on for eternity.

I have but one request, my love, and that is: Please take care of Mom. She means the world to me and has been with me every step of the way. I wouldn't be here if it hadn't been for her. She loves you, baby, and is so happy we found each other again. She has been our biggest cheerleader, fighting for us since the beginning. I know it hasn't been easy with all of us adjusting to sharing our lives together, but please always remember how much you mean to her and know how proud she is that you are in her little's girl's life. You must be one special man, my love, for Mom to be so content and completely secure in the fact that, no matter what, her little girl will be safe, loved and taken care of. She knows it's okay to let go of me, knowing I'm in good hands.

There is only one thing I want for you, babe, and that is for you to be happy. After all I've been through, I've realized how precious life is and how easily it can be taken away. Don't ever take your life for granted, Kevin. You are so immensely blessed. Remember everything we've discovered together and how you've grown to understand yourself. I love you, I cherish you and I am so blessed to call you mine. I want to spend the rest of my life loving you and making you happy. Please know that I will always be with you, no matter what.

Yours always and forever,
Tina xoxo

P.S. I sent a letter for Mom to your email but it's only to be given to her if... well, you know.

CHAPTER THIRTEEN
There's No Place Like Home

Every detail of my case was scrutinized and my health history, as well as my current physical condition, was taken into consideration. Decisions were finalized during a three-hour pre-operation appointment with the Chief of Anesthesiology, Dr. C. There had been some major screw-ups in the past, but I felt calm while waiting to be wheeled into the operating room. Laying on a stretcher outside of the operating room, the anesthesiologist on duty approached the bed and asked: "Is there any medical history I should be aware of?"

I could not believe what I was hearing; this had to be a dream. The anesthesiologist had absolutely no knowledge of what was discussed during the pre-op appointment or the plan of action options for pain management. He had not even glanced at my chart. Taking the chart, he flipped through the pages and immediately decided that he would be doing a spinal for the procedure. I quickly explained my long-standing issues with chronic pain, my health history and my current health problems, and I informed him about what Dr. C and I had discussed. I also told him that after speaking with my physician, weighing all of my options and taking Dr. C's "avoid wind-up at all costs" advice, anesthesia would be best during surgery, with a pain pump for post-surgical pain management.

After fourteen years of taking high doses of narcotics, in addition to the many procedures and surgeries I had endured, I was extremely tolerant to medications and would not react to them like the average person. It seemed that he did not hear a single word I said, and concluded that a spinal was the best thing to do. He didn't even mention the post-surgical plan as he rolled me into surgery. I began to panic when I realized that a spinal meant that I would be awake during the surgery. There was no way I was going to be awake while my stomach muscles were being ripped apart and my reproductive organs were being removed, even if I couldn't feel anything.

I demanded that he give me something so that I would not be aware of what was happening. The nurse held me in a sitting position and restrained me while he pushed the needle into my spine. I wanted to run out of there as fast as I possibly could, and she knew it. I saw the surgeon holding the scalpel and soon felt the pressure in my abdomen as he made the first cut. With tears falling down the sides of my face, I looked up at the anesthesiologist standing above me and begged for help. I felt terrified and helpless as I screamed, "Please stop!" That was my last memory, and in what seemed like minutes, I awoke in the recovery room.

I cannot begin to describe the excruciating pain I awoke to. Obviously, this wasn't my first experience with extreme pain; however, this was intolerable. The nurses did all they could with the only medication they were permitted to administer, Dilautid. But they could not bring about even a hint of relief. I was now in full pain "wind-up." In layman's terms, this means the pain is way past the point of no return. After a few hours of agony they decided to call the anesthesiologist. It took another hour or so for him to show up and advise the nurses to attach a pain pump.

I had repeatedly vomited all over myself, kicked off the blankets and screamed for the nurses to get Mom and Kevin, who were right on the other side of the huge silver door in front of me. I had not taken my regular pain medication prior to the surgery, which was now long overdue. The symptoms became even more unbearable, but the nurses refused to get my pain meds from Mom or Kevin. They certainly didn't want my loved ones seeing me like this.

After perusing my chart again, the anesthesiologist agreed to administer the dose of OxyContin that I had been taking for years.

The hospital pharmacy only had 10mg tablets, so they decided to send someone to another pharmacy to fetch 80mg tablets, instead of opening that silver door and getting them from Mom or Kevin. I was stunned. There I was, screaming in agony with a pain pump attached to my neck. The nurse yelled at me to stop moving, exclaiming that this was the only vein that hadn't collapsed. I just couldn't understand how this had happened when we had taken every precaution possible. I continued to vomit repeatedly.

I vaguely remember being moved to a bed in a dimly-lit room and seeing Kevin and Mom looking down at me, their faces filled with concern. It had been at least twelve hours since they'd seen me last. I whispered that I was okay as I faded away. I awoke to the sound of a heart monitor, but the rhythm seemed to be way too fast, which made me open my eyes. I saw a young girl with a big belly in the bed beside mine. I was in the maternity ward. Tiny little heartbeats, crying babies and the sounds of happy parents surrounded me as I buried my head under the blankets trying to subdue the noises. I couldn't move without wincing. I was stuck there.

I desperately wanted children; I had always wanted to be a mom. And here I was in the maternity ward after having a sub-total hysterectomy. How could this be? I had booked a semi-private room during my pre-op to avoid this altogether, but here I was. Kevin, Mom and Kody came to see me early that morning and could obviously see the distress on my face. They knew what was causing it without me mentioning it. I continued to assure them that I was fine.

Later that night I could no longer stand it. At approximately 2:00 a.m., I got myself out of bed, wheeled the IV pole and pain pump down the corridors to the elevator, and made my way outside. I spent just shy of two hours sitting on a bench, absolutely devastated. "Be the witness, Tina, not the participant!" I repeatedly heard in my mind. But couldn't try in the least.

The pain management team came to see me often. They profusely apologized for everything that had occurred, including putting me in the maternity ward. They were compassionate and also very curious as to how I had maintained such a dose of narcotics for fifteen years without having to increase it due to tolerance. I explained that I would wean myself down to 160mg daily every couple of years. Their looks of astonishment made me giggle loudly; they couldn't grasp how I had done this.

There is no cure or prevention for tolerance, so this was the only way I could do it. The physical withdrawals from OxyContin weren't a big deal to me, and I was easily weaned over eight weeks or so. Of course the pain was unmanaged during these periods, so it required a lot of meditation, as well as breakthrough medication, but my focus on "quality of life," which Dr. B had so beautifully taught me, was pivotal. This weaning procedure allowed me to never have to go any higher than 480mg twice daily, thus avoiding the undesirable side effects of higher doses. The three pain management specialists took notes on this. They were fascinated not only by my discovery, but by my willingness to even try such a thing. They thanked me for being so amazing, which made me chuckle.

My surgeon was sitting on the side of my bed, gently holding my hand. He explained that, despite the surgery, I never would have been able to have children. My uterus was deformed and hard like a walnut. He said we did the right thing. He asked if I had ever had a miscarriage, which brought back the memory of losing Kevin's baby all those years ago. Tears sprang to my eyes once again as I vividly remembered the blood. There was so much blood! It was all over the sheets and the mattress of our bed. I had lost a baby. I had lost Kevin's baby. The surgeon wiped my tears away with the back of his hand and asked if there was anything he could do. Indeed there was. He could discharge me and let me go home.

With a look of concern he explained that the pain pump was still needed and I would have to be weaned, and furthermore, that I could not climb stairs under any circumstances or lift anything heavier than five pounds for three months. I laughed at his concern regarding weaning me from the pain pump, telling him that I was a pro and this pump could be removed immediately without issue.

I then reassured him that I had a strong loving boyfriend at home who would happily carry me everywhere I needed to go, and that with Mom's support I would be just fine... much better than I would be here in the maternity ward. He quickly apologized, explaining that there was absolutely nowhere else to put me, and that it had disturbed him upon hearing that this was the last available bed. All I could feel was compassion for him and a deep sense of gratitude as I told him I just wanted to be at home with my family. I promised I would be extra careful.

"There's no place like home!" came out of my mouth as soon as I was back in my own bed, with Kevin beside me and Mom doing everything she could to make me comfortable. I was weak and sore, but happy it was all over. The head of the bed was positioned all the way up vertical, just the way it had to be. I loved the feeling of clean crisp sheets caressing my skin. As I laid my head back against the pillow, the memories of the visualizations I had done prior to the surgery came rushing back. Although the journey had been a little bumpier than I'd expected, the outcome was the one I desired, and I couldn't help but smile. My heart was heavy from revisiting the memory of losing our baby, but I was still here and thankful for every single breath.

Kevin never left my side as we watched movie after movie. Mom brought me all my favorite juices mixed with Kent's miraculous concoctions, followed by the custom multi-vitamins he had made for me. Yes, I was more than grateful that I was here to live this moment, surrounded by such unconditional and unwavering love.

The next few months went by like clockwork, and with meditation I healed quickly. My three-month follow-up with the surgeon went smoothly. He bragged about his artwork, as there was only a tiny little white scar on my lower abdomen. Of course I had to praise him, but I also informed him of the amazing magic of a good skin care regimen. This made us both laugh. He was pleased with my progress and announced that I could resume my care under the guidance of Dr. Buckley, upon which we said our goodbyes.

My blood work results were back. Dr. Buckley explained that the bio-identical hormone medications had to be increased, along with a few others, but that I was doing well under the circumstances. It was now time to revisit the hip and lower back issues, but I was in no rush; I would give my body time to re-adjust. I also needed to allow time to resolve the pain wind-up before making any further decisions. This had certainly taken its toll as evidenced by my cortisol (stress hormone) level, which was much too high.

I never left the bedroom , but not once was I ever made to feel less than. I also no longer felt less than, so this wasn't refected back to me anymore. I had to stay in bed– big deal. It didn't change the fact of what I truly was and would always be... perfect and whole.

Diary Entry, September 2011

Reading Dr. L's emails have again thrown me for a loop and I don't know what to do. I don't ever want to take those horrible medications again. I must admit, I'm a little bewildered as to why he is recommending them, and also—why all the caps?

Email from Dr. L, Dated April 1, 2011

WELL! WELL! WELL!

AGAIN... THESE GUYS ARE PATCHING THE EFFECTS OF THE CAUSE, FIDDLING AROUND, BUT NOT GIVING THE DIAGNOSIS OF COMPLETE EXHAUSTION OF ALL SYSTEMS DUE TO PAIN AND THE MORAL CONSEQUENCES OF ALL FAILURES. IT'S CALLED THALAMIC, HYPO-THALAMIC, PITUITARY, END-ORGAN FAILURE AGAIN. THIS MECHANISM IS NOT KNOWN BY 99% OF THE MEDICAL BODY. I FOUND OUT LAST WEEK A SUGGESTION FOR TREATING THIS WITH A LOW DOSE OF STEROIDS. THIS IS SOMETHING I'VE KNOWN FOR OVER 12 YEARS, GETTING IT FROM A CLINIC IN NORTH CAROLINA SPECIALIZING IN TREATING FIBROMYALGIA. AND IT IS A SPECIFIC

CLASS OF ADRENAL STEROIDS!!!??!!! FOOD FOR THOUGHT, HEY?

YOU'RE NOT TREATED. YOU THINK THAT ANALGESICS WILL TAKE CARE OF EVERYTHING, BUT YOU FORGOT TO PROTECT YOUR BRAIN FROM ITS INTERNAL DAMAGE. AND YOU'RE NOT IN A POSITION TO MONITOR THAT DAMAGE. HAVE YOU LOST ALONG THE WAY THE NOTION OF A PLAN— A MULTIFACETED PLAN, AND INSTEAD FOCUSED ON MARGINAL ISSUES? THE PROOF IS IN THE PUDDING. OXYCONTIN AND DIAZEPAM ONLY?

BY ALL REFERENCES, YOU'RE ON THE DOWN-SLOPE. ANY REVIEW OF YOUR MEDICAL CHART WILL CONCLUDE THE SAME.

MIND YOU, EVEN MY PERSONAL PHYSICIAN DEALING WITH PAIN DOESN'T GET INVOLVED WITH TREATING NEUROPATHIC PAIN. WHAT ABOUT KETAMINE? THEY DON'T KNOW ABOUT IT IN CANADA? IT'S THE MOST POWERFUL BLOCKER ON THE NMDA RECEPTOR! SO WHERE TO START TO HELP YOU?

YOU'RE TRYING TO CORRECT THE END RESULTS OF AN OVERSTRAINED NERVOUS SYSTEM, BUT NOT ADDRESSING THE CORE, ONLY THE PERIPH-ERALS. IT WON'T WORK.

AREAS TO LOOK AT:

1)   PROTECTING THE THOUGHT PROCESS WITH ANTI-DEPRESSANTS: ZOLOFT (SERTRALINE) OR CIPRALEX (ESCITALOPRAM)

2)   PROTECTING THE CENTRAL NERVOUS SYSTEM: ELAVIL (AMITRYPTYLINE)

3)   REDUCING THE PAIN INPUT IN THE BRAIN: NEURONTIN (GABAPENTIN) OR LYRICA (PREGABALIN)

4)   APPROPRIATE PERIPHERAL PAIN BLOCKAGE: ALTERNATING THE NARCOTICS; THERE ARE NEW MEDS IN THE LAST 6 MONTHS; TARGIN, BUTRIN, AND THERE IS THE 3-DAY PAIN PROTECTION FROM DURAGESIC (FENTANYL) PATCHES. TARGIN AND BUTRIN ARE NOT YET REIMBURSED BY INSURANCE, MOST PROBABLY.

5)   MENTAL RECUPERATION AS WELL AS MENTAL PROTECTION OVERNIGHT? RESTORIL (CLONAZEPAM) OR IMOVANE (ZOPICLONE)

A WOUND NEEDS MANY APPROACHES, RIGHT? WISDOM WILL NOT ENHANCE WOUND HEALING , NO MATTER HOW MUCH YOU TRY!

MOST PHYSICIANS WILL NOT TOUCH YOU WITH A TEN-FOOT POLE, EVEN TO THE POINT OF POLITELY REJECTING YOU BY ALL SORTS OF DEMEANOR.

THE WORST IS THAT YOU'VE BEEN GIVEN WRONG EXPLANATIONS ABOUT YOUR CONDITION, AND THAT YOU MIGHT BE RELYING ONLY ON EVENTUAL SURGERIES.

AT PRESENT, THE SUGGESTED TREATMENT IS RADIO-FREQUENCY ABLATION OF THE DISC, AND IT IS NOT AVAILABLE IN OTTAWA.

REMEMBER THE NEUROLOGIST WHO RECOMMENDED ME TO SEND YOU TORONTO, NOT EVEN KNOWING ANYTHING ABOUT THE PROCEDURE!!!!

WHY NOT CHEMONUCLEOLYSIS? NOBODY KNOWS ABOUT THAT PROCEDURE AROUND HERE.

MY LAST CONVERSATION ABOUT THAT PROCEDURE (THAT I SUBMITTED MYSELF TO IN 1975????) WAS ABOUT 8 YEARS AGO.

AND, I AM VERY TROUBLED THAT EVERYBODY
IS FOCUSING ON THE ANNULOUS TEAR!!!!

SO? I GUESS YOU'LL HAVE TO GO TO CONFESSION,
'FAIRE TES PÂQUES' AND THEN MAKE SOME
DECISIONS. OF COURSE, PAST EXPERIENCES WITH
MEDICATION WILL HAVE TO BE TAKEN INTO
ACCOUNT AND RESPECTED.

Dr. L

Diary Entry, November 2011

Dr. L and I are not even in the same ballpark anymore, and it's time to part ways. I can 't keep listening to this; it just doesn't resonate with me at all and it hasn't in years. "Wisdom will not enhance wound healing no matter how hard you try." What is he talking about? This is a projection and nothing less, since all he boasts about is how wise he is. It makes me laugh every time I'm told that I'm dying. I can't help but reply, "So are you. We all are. None of us are getting out of here alive." It's just that I have the blessing of knowing it and not taking anything for granted, which makes every moment of every day absolutely miraculous. I have constant reminders to savor every single day, regardless of the form they take. And above all to love... to love madly, fiercely and completely.

Do I just sit in bed day after day and let my life pass me by, or do I make the decision for surgery? I want to go out with Kevin, enjoy adventures together and have a normal life. I want to take Mom to Vegas, on the trip of a lifetime and spoil her rotten. What do I do?

Kevin never complains, and holds my hand every step of the way. I love him so much, but does he not deserve more? Mom never utters a word of disappointment but I know things could be so much better for all of us. I'm just not sure how to get there. We are blessed, this is I know, but I have dreams.

Meditating daily and savoring each moment is of course providing great quality of life, but should I consider surgery with the slightest hope of improvement? I must speak with Dr. Buckley about taking over all my medical care and ask Dr. B to guide her, as this is his expertise. I can no longer stay under Dr. L's care; this should have come to an end long ago. With Dr. B and Dr. Buckley I will be in the best of hands, with doctors who have the same mindset—that everything is possible.

Before I consider going under the knife again I'm going to lower my dose of OxyContin until I'm at 80mg twice daily. Then I will continue until I'm off of it totally, lowering the risk of anesthesia and giving my body the break it needs. This is going to be challenging, but with meditation it is certainly doable. The physical withdrawals aren't a big deal; I'm not worried in the least about that, since I've done it countless times. It's the inevitable increase in pain symptoms that is going to be tough. I must remember my new definition of pain as it increases over the next few months and remain the witness in every moment without judgment, opinion, bias, or belief. I can do this!

I will temporarily move into the spare bedroom so I can get through the night sweats and chills without Kevin having to watch. He's working now, so I don't want to keep him up all night. At least during the day it will just be Mom and me, and she's seen this many times before. This will take some time, but I'm a pro and know exactly what to do.

This completely resonates with me; I'm actually excited to get started... so yes, this must be right. Anything that has excited me in the past has brought about doubts, obstacles and fears, but by standing my ground and keeping my focus on the dream, it has always beautifully manifested itself; every single time.

The thought of having a capable and pain-free body fills me with such joy and such bliss—that is my ultimate dream. As I'm sitting here writing this, I'm literally feeling as if I already do, and I'm imagining all the wonderful adventures I'm experiencing with the people I love. Hiking, walking, traveling, eating and loving. Living my calling, sharing my journey along with my discoveries, speaking publicly, being an "in your face" extreme example that everything is possible, and helping others remember what they truly are. What more could I ask for? *(End of diary entry.)*

CHAPTER FOURTEEN
Goodbyes are Never Easy

The last few months had not been easy, but I was getting there. Every cut in dosage was followed by three nights of sweating, shivering, and tossing and turning. It felt similar to a rake being dragged across my back, making me cringe. I was used to these symptoms since I had done this many times before to control tolerance and maintain my quality of life without ever having to exceed my maximum comfortable dose. So in hindsight, it wasn't that bad. I know Kevin and Mom worried, but I had to do this on my own, as I always had, and an audience wasn't appreciated.

I wondered if I was causing them to worry by hiding the severity of my symptoms and always insisting I was perfectly fine—even when I was going through the worst of it. I would put a smile on my face and convince them that everything was awesome, that I was doing great and there was nothing to worry about. It was obvious that they could see the toll this was taking on me. Being honest with them and sharing the brutal realities felt like complaining, and I felt that it would only perpetuate the actual feelings associated with having to go through something like this. They never truly knew the extent of what I was going through, which perhaps caused mistrust and worry, but I knew I had this. I was the same way with my doctors. My focus was on the dream. My energy was wrapped up in imaginings of living that dream, and that's the way I preferred it. I never lost sight of my dream.

Once I reached a dose of 200mg every twelve hours, I decided to take a break and take Mom to Las Vegas for the trip of a lifetime. VIP all the way, of course! I booked the Garth Brooks VIP Getaway package at the Wynn Encore Hotel, complete with a private elevator and concierge, and front row tickets to Garth's acoustic concert. We also had tickets to Cirque Du Soleil's "O," a breathtaking performance in a theatre custom-built for this production. I wanted to make Mom's biggest dream come true— Vegas with a load of money to play the slot machines. And she would be insanely pampered with spa days and scrumptious dinners, as well. Kevin was ecstatic, encouraging me to go all-out. And I did. Everything was booked and we were soon on the plane to live Mom's dream. We couldn't have been more excited.

I won't go into too much detail, but although Mom caught a horrible virus, we were still able to thoroughly enjoy the Garth Brooks concert, as well as some of the spa services. She even won a little bit of money. We spent the rest of our holiday in the hotel room, as Mom was unable to get out of bed. She was on oxygen the entire plane ride home.

Upon arrival back home, Mom was brought directly to the hospital and admitted. I was exhausted and terrified. It was so weird to have us both being pushed around in wheelchairs at the airport. Seeing her so sick and helpless, I thought about what she must have witnessed firsthand for the last fifteen years or so in having to take care of me. This was heart wrenching. Not in a million years would I have traded places with her and gone through what she had. I had experienced nothing compared to her.

After we returned from Vegas, I resumed the detox from the OxyContin. I was determined and excited to get down to 40mg every twelve hours, so I was cutting doses much more quickly than I had before. This was uncomfortable, to say the least. Especially with traveling back and forth to London to spend time with my cousin Danielle, who was going through her journey with ALS. I knew she was nearing the end of that journey, and I wanted to spend as much time with her as possible. She had been there for me and I was certainly going to be there for her.

That August, I received a phone call from my godmother, Aunt Sue, letting me know that Danielle had decided to end life support. I knew exactly what had to be done, as I had been there myself. Mom and I took off immediately for the five-hour drive and we were soon at Danielle's side in the hospital.

We had spent a lot of time with our precious Danielle over the last few years, and we had many conversations on this subject. She was with me when I was dying, and she had been a major contributor to ensuring we focused on the celebration of life, the sharing of memories and the absolute need for laughter. I was now getting the chance to return the favor. Although Danielle could no longer speak, we used a letter board to communicate as she blinked her eyes in response. When I asked if there was anything she was afraid of, the word "suffering" was her response. I was going to do everything possible, and then some, to prevent her from suffering in any way.

It seemed long and drawn out, but needless to say, Danielle didn't suffer in the least. And because I was speaking to the medical staff, everything was always taken care of. We all had our private time with her, giving us a chance to say what we needed to say. I asked her if there was anything she wanted from me; if she had any last wishes, and using the board, she spelled out "Sedona." It took me a while to figure this out, but I finally realized she wanted some of her ashes brought to the Red Rock vortex in Sedona, where she had first discovered her connection to the One and had felt the breathtaking power within her. This was a promise she knew I would keep.

Danielle was always astonished and inspired by my spirit and by my absolute willingness to redefine everything that provoked a negative feeling. As a former police officer with the RCMP, she understood trauma and was fascinated that I had literally rewritten history with regard to any memory flashes that used to haunt me. She was in complete fascination, and hoped that I would one day share this with the many others who suffer from PTSD and teach them that they indeed had the ability to take back their power.

Danielle understood more than most the toll of a long drawn-out illness, and she knew that I was tired. It had been nine years since I'd eaten solid food, eleven years since I had a bowel movement on my own, and sixteen years since the accident. Alone in that hospital room with her, I had a request of my own. I told her that if I got any worse in the next two years, and my spirit was dwindling, I wanted her to come and get me and bring me to heaven with her. Her eyes opened wide upon hearing my request; I knew she was thinking of Kevin and Mom. I explained that I was happy beyond belief and loved more than I could ever fathom, but that I didn't know how much more I had in me. She blinked in agreement. I sobbed as I held her, knowing she was holding me back with her heart. She understood exactly why I had made such a request, as only she could.

I told everyone to go home, get some rest, and that I would stay with Danielle. Holding her hand as I looked at her, I could tell that she was at peace. I could feel it. With tears streaming down my face, I couldn't help but be happy for her, knowing that this journey of ALS was coming to an end and that she had a new beginning.

When the respiratory therapist walked in and turned her CPAP machine off, I was stunned. I sat there frozen for over five minutes, not knowing what to do. Everyone had left. I looked at Danielle intently, and I knew she was gone. The therapist suddenly realized that Danielle's parents weren't in the room, and said, "Maybe you should call the family," as he turned the breathing machine back on. I frantically called Aunt Sue and Uncle Danny. I knew Danielle was already gone, but I couldn't make myself utter the words. They wanted to be with her at the end, I'm sure. There were no heart monitors or machines in the room to indicate that she had passed, and watching the breathing machine inflate her lungs was too much to bear. Mom and I returned to our hotel room where I tearfully told her what had happened. We were grateful that Danielle was at peace now, and we held each other tightly.

Back at the hospital just before midnight, they called time of death, but the stiffness of her body made it obvious that she had died hours ago. I held Aunt Sue as she loved on her daughter, and I comforted Uncle Danny, her brother Brad and her best friend Heather as well as I could. Should I tell them? No, this was not the time.

As I walked up to the stage at the memorial to give my eulogy, the sight of the crowd took my breath away. Many dozens of people dressed in beautiful, vibrant colors filled the room, and her friends and colleagues from the Royal Canadian Mounted Police were dressed in the red serge full dress uniform. This was Danielle; she was every vivid color in existence. She was exceptional, loving, adventurous, strong and independent. She was Danielle, and her spirit would live on forever in our hearts. She had made such an impact on everyone who had the privilege of knowing her and had touched immeasurable lives along the way. I treasure her. I think of her often, and always with a smile. I knew she would be with me in spirit to help me the rest of the way with detox.

By the middle of April 2013, I was down to 60mg of OxyContin every twelve hours. I knew something was drastically wrong due to the extreme pain in my face. The pain became obvious at 120mg, but I refused to acknowledge it.

With every reduction in pain medication , the face pain worsened. I continued to detox, getting to a dose of 80mg daily, but I could no longer stay in denial of the pain; it was unbearable. I had to tell Mom and Kevin. Just walking through the house, I had to put my hands in front of my face to block the air, as even air flow on my face caused intense sharp pain. A slight touch, or even a teardrop, brought me to my knees. I had also lost vision in my left eye and was having difficulty swallowing. It felt like there were a million knives stabbing my face and head. This resulted in awful bouts of vomiting. The burning in my throat was constant and relentless, which further contributed to the difficulty in swallowing.

On the third anniversary of our fateful loved-filled reunion at the airport in Alberta, Kevin dropped to one knee beside the bed where I spent all of my time, and with the most beautiful box in his hand, he tearfully said, "I've loved you forever and always will. Will you finally make me the happiest man in the world?"

Despite the pain, I leapt into his arms screaming, "Yes!" I was desperately trying not to cry; I could not believe that I was finally going to be married to the love of my life. I had scrolled "Tina Blackwell" all over my binders in high school and now I was finally going to be Tina Blackwell.

The love I feel for this man is not of this world. It is unconditional, unending and limitless, with a passion so intense, it is overwhelming. I was going to be married to my first love, finally. As we held each other tightly, I looked up at Danielle's hat hanging on the wall. I knew she was with us. In my mind's eye, I saw the biggest smile on her face. I opened the box, and the beauty of the ring, the sparkle of the diamond and the look on Kevin's face made me gasp. He carefully placed the ring on my finger—the very same finger on which we each had wedding bands tattooed within days of reuniting. Dreams do come true, they really do!

The next few months were spent trying to find answers to the cause of the debilitating pain in my face, the diminishment of eye sight in my left eye, and now the bruising and swelling in my forehead and cheeks. After visits with three specialists and multiple three-dimensional images, the cause was found. And I was dumbfounded.

It turns out, a dentist I had seen ten years prior had broken a root canal drill during the procedure, left it in my gum, and covered it up with a temporary crown. Due to the high amounts of pain medications I was taking, I was completely unaware of it until I was at a low enough dose to actually feel the pain. A minimum of eight surgeries would be required, all of them under anesthesia—beginning immediately.

I knew the risks of anesthesia in my case, but unfortunately this time, Mom and Kevin were also privy to this information. Due to my current state of health and my history, the odds were 50/50 with anesthesia. It took such a massive amount of anesthesia to put me under that the risk of death was high. I somehow knew everything would be okay... and so did my love.

Kevin and I were with Dr. Buckley as I told her everything we had discovered, what had to be done, and of course the risks with anesthesia—not that she didn't already know. Her strength, conviction and unconditional love and support in that moment meant more than I could ever express. I knew she would be here waiting after this was all over with, as she had always been. I was so blessed to have her as my doctor, and also as my friend. She had also accepted Kevin as a patient and I couldn't have been more thankful for the love she had shown him. Before leaving, I gave her an extra-long hug. Then I made my way to Laura, the Body Chemistry Balancing coordinator at NutriChem™ for another loving embrace.

Five days prior to the first surgery, Kevin and I went down to the church to be married. Mom and Kody were our witnesses, and my wonderful cousin, Andre, surprised us by coming to take photos of the wedding. On September 10th, 2013 at 2:00 p.m., a Tuesday afternoon, Kevin and I became husband and wife in the most breathtaking ceremony I have ever experienced.

Although my face was swollen and covered in black/red bruises, I felt like the most beautiful bride in the refection from Kevin's eyes. I had tried to cover up the bruises with special makeup that my cousin Julie had suggested, but one stroke of the brush made my legs give out beneath me as I screamed in agony. Standing here looking into my love's eyes, there was no need to cover anything up. He saw who I truly was, he always had, and he knew me to the depths of my being.

He lovingly held my hands, giving them a squeeze every so often to prevent me from crying, knowing the pain of a single tear on my cheek was excruciating. He lovingly looked at me, reassuring me in every moment that we would indeed have years to share together. This wasn't the end, it was just the beginning. Looking back at him, there was nothing more I wished for. "I now pronounce you husband and wife," the pastor said, as I jumped to finally kiss my husband. I knew those lips.

There was joyous laughter from everyone and the most loving expression on Mom's face. This was also her dream come true. Her little girl was here to live this moment. I will never forget the happiest day of my life and indeed it was, regardless of the circumstances or the state I was in. I had dreamed of this day since I was sixteen years old.

When I weakened, Kevin got stronger. When Kevin weakened, I got stronger. When we both weakened, Mom was strong enough for both of us. We were facing one hell of a journey, but we were doing it together. Mom wasn't alone anymore to sit in the waiting room for hours on end, worrying that she might never see her little girl again. She had Kevin by her side, who never once faltered in the belief that I was going to be just fine; that we were going to grow old and grey together. Mom wasn't alone anymore; she was with my Kevin, my love, and she couldn't have been in better hands. They had each other for strength and comfort and I was immensely grateful. I was so blessed to be loved by such extraordinary human beings. One I had the privilege of calling "Mom," and the other I had the privilege of calling "my husband." My husband... it still tugs at my heart strings and brings tears to my eyes.

I can't help thinking of Mom sitting in those grim waiting rooms all by herself, watching helplessly when I was sick, bedridden and desperately trying to recover. She had to do this on her own for fourteen years, and I couldn't imagine how she had remained so strong and positive. I guess she didn't have a choice.

Kevin and Mom spent the days following my surgery looking after me and thoroughly reviewing the information given to them by the specialists regarding post-anesthesia complications, symptoms, and what to watch for. There were no hospital stays after the surgeries; I was coming home immediately. So the responsibility was on them for 24-hour care after each one. The surgeries would be weekly until they were all completed. We had a long road ahead of us.

My brother Marc came to visit, and I was so happy to see him. He did really well in controlling his emotions upon seeing the state I was in. I looked like a raccoon with a really big forehead. This visual made me want to giggle, although I couldn't even smile. He walked over to my bed and gently put his arms around me. Even now, as I sit here writing this, the clean smell of his white t-shirt and his wonderful cologne fill the air around me. How I loved my big brother. He had always been my hero and he still is. His hug that day made me feel like everything was okay, that I was safe and that I was loved. I don't have much more recollection about that week, other than feeling anxious for the surgeries to begin so that some relief would finally come. I couldn't take much more. I had never experienced such torturous and unrelenting pain. I hoped to God that it would be alleviated by the surgeries.

Email correspondence titled "Unbelievable" between Dr. B and me, dated September 11, 2010:

Hi Dr. B,

You are never going to believe this. I couldn't believe it, but everything has finally sunk in. Last March, after getting through most of the detox, I began to feel severe pain in my mouth, especially when I got down to 40mg/12hrs. I went to see a dentist, who sent me to another dentist, and both finally disclosed that the work was above their expertise. I was then sent to a periodontist, who referred me to an endodontist. I'm telling you, we were anxious to find out what was going on. By the time I got in to see the endodontist, my face was black and swollen. My eyes, forehead, nose, temples, and right cheek were all black and I felt pain all over my face and head. The vision in my left eye was diminished and I was having trouble swallowing.

The endodontist informed me that a root canal drill bit had been left in the root by another dentist. It migrated through the tip of the root and the ligaments, and was lodged near the cheekbone. There is a lot of infection and the damage is severe. Due to the location of this drill, the trigeminal nerve is innervated, causing the pain and other symptoms (twitching, swelling, etc.). He explained that this nerve is the largest in the body and has twelve branches.

It's the maxillary branch that is most affected, and as I'm sure you know, it is affecting all of the other branches as well.

That appointment was at the end of July, so this has been a long journey. I will finally return this Monday for the first surgery. I have to be under anesthesia for all of the surgeries. The endodontist will remove the drill bit, inject antibiotics, and take a tissue sample from the roof of my mouth to rebuild the root. That's the first surgery. On the second appointment, he will complete two root canals, once the root tip has healed. After this, I must see the periodontist to continue the last of the surgeries.

The last dentist I saw was ten years ago—the one who broke the drill bit and didn't even bother to remove it or complete the root canal. He just fused one crown beside another one to cover up his screw-up. At that time, he knew of all the medications I was taking, and both of us believed that I would be taking these medications for the rest of my life. I guess he figured I wouldn't feel it and he'd get away with it.

Implants or dentures are not possible due to the amount of bone loss. Therefore, root canals, filing down the teeth, then covering them with crowns is our only option. But this will only last a maximum of ten years. The infection is severe and we've tried antibiotics, but the specialist told us that the only way to get at this infection is by going directly to the source, then removing the drill bit. It all begins Monday, thank God. Both specialists are working together and there will be a minimum of eight surgeries. They are also bringing in an anesthesiologist.

I must say, Dr. B, that I thank God I detoxed off the OxyContin when I did; it must have been fate. I am staying strong and positive with daily meditation and of course positive affirmations. This pain is nothing like I have ever experienced. It is intense to say the least, but I am coping. I am taking 40mg of OxyContin every twelve hours and 4mg of Dilautid twice daily for breakthrough. It is helping, but I don 't think anything can really numb this pain in the slightest... I'm very grateful for meditation.

Sincerely, Tina xo

P.S. Kevin and I were married yesterday. It was so beautiful, Dr. B. You should have seen my mom. xo

Response from Dr. B

Hello Tina,

This is indeed truly unbelievable. You can write a book about this someday.

All the best with your recovery. I think you have paid your dues for several lifetimes...

Congratulations to you and Kevin.

Kindest regards, Dr. B

Diary Entry, September 15, 2013

Whether something is a tragedy or a blessing is not defined by the event or occurrence; the definition lies within you. It is a choice you must repeatedly make, and there is only one choice: Yes or No. Choose wisely, and don't let the ego deceive you. Yes or No, Love or Fear... that is the choice. Suffering and hurting are optional in life. Repeatedly, just make the conscious choice to say Yes to whatever comes. Open your heart to whatever the now brings, and spread your wings and fly. Once the heart is open, the mind will follow. Be the witness instead of the participant, knowing that the only limitations you have are those you place upon yourself.

Drop your judgments, opinions and biases and set yourself free. You won't ever know how strong you are until being strong is the only choice. Once discovered, you know beyond a shadow of a doubt that there is nothing you can't do, that you are limitless. Regardless of what life sends you, you've got this. Truly knowing how powerful you are is the greatest gift; there are no victims in life. Don't resist the tests, they are teachers, and only you get to mark your own scoresheet. You and you alone. That is the gift.

Don't be fooled into believing you're a victim; they do not exist. The ego is slowly learning this, but it will choose all kinds of "How could they?" or "How could this?" to avoid that realization and refuel itself. Know that you, and you alone, pay for the gas, so put your money away. It's always up to you. There is nothing you can't change by shining brighter—NOTHING! This includes any situation or circumstance. And the greatest blessing of all is that your entire existence changes. YOU change! You become pure love, and you can then see how everything that happens in life happens *for* you, as you respond with wide-open arms and gratitude. There is no greater state of being than pure love, and you deserve nothing less... as do I.

How can I see this any other way than as a gift? How can I see anything in my life as anything other than a gift? I am saying Yes, utterly and completely, without defining or judging my situation. I am fully aware of the "facts" or the "odds," but I don't have to believe them. My beliefs create my reality. Therefore I believe this is just another beautiful journey leading to awe, bliss and the realization that I am beyond limitation. I am awe, bliss, pure love. I am limitless, with my wings in full expansion. I am the magic I wish to feel in the world.

My journey awaits. Excitement fills every cell of my body as I imagine the adventure ahead. I see love, I am love, it's all love. I've given up on someone or something needing to be lovable before I love them. Yes, I am love. This physical body has nothing to do with what I am; this is yet another signpost guiding my way. I will not waste one moment in worry or fear. I'm allowing the current to carry me, and I'm enjoying one hell of a ride!

I am so blessed to have such magnificent reminders of the being I am. I am so blessed to be loved by Kevin and Mom. God, I know you've got this, so what is there for me to fret about? This state of trust and faith fills me with the highest of vibrations. Honestly, maintaining my alignment is the only thing I ever have to do and that is exactly what I'm doing. I'm happy, in love, and at peace. I'm saying Yes in every moment. I am so blessed.

Sitting here knowing I'm heading into my first of many surgeries in the morning, I know that no one and nothing outside of myself is responsible for how I feel. No person, situation or circumstance is ever responsible for my state of being... ever. If I can make such a bold statement , anyone can. This is exciting. I can actually choose to feel "blissed out," no matter what... and I really am. How cool is that? *(End of diary entry.)*

CHAPTER FIFTEEN
Under the Knife and Under the Gun

The four months it took to complete the nine surgeries are mostly a blur. I'm sure Mom and Kevin could tell you much more, but I do recall the 45-minute drive to Ottawa the morning of the first surgery. I had been instructed to take these little pills in the tiniest envelope I'd ever seen one hour prior to surgery. They were sedatives, I believe, since I was totally mellowed out.

I remember lying in a dental chair feeling pretty comfy. The endodontist was on my right and his assistant was on my left. I recall briefly seeing the anesthesiologist before I was off to la la land. I had a flash of waking up mid-surgery with my mouth full of equipment, trying to convince the doctor and his assistant to fall in love, that they were beautiful and meant to be together, before I faded out again. This makes me giggle to this day. I wonder if they ever took my advice? Even under anesthesia I was still in love with love.

I'll never forget waking up to the look of shock on the anesthesiologist's face as he proceeded to tell me that I was the most tolerant human to anesthesia medications he had ever encountered. He told me he could have knocked out ten men with what it took to get this little girl under. This was not a surprise to me; I had heard it many times in the last seventeen years.

Beams of bright light piercing the darkness, hands on my chest and the feeling of warmth against my face—these are the only memories I have following each surgery. Mom and Kevin took turns every fifteen minutes throughout the night to ensure I was still breathing, coming into my "healing room" with flashlights, since the windows were blacked out. Kevin had to work early in the mornings, but this didn't stop him. Even though Mom had offered to take it on, he wouldn't hear of it. The sense of comfort, love and safety in my state of complete vulnerability and haze cannot be expressed. I knew they were there and I was so happy to be home with them instead of in some hospital.

Mom would pour liquids mixed with Kent's NutriChem™ powders into my mouth during the days and spoon feed me whatever I would agree to. She followed this with the custom mutli-vitamin capsules NutriChem™ had prepared for me, which kept me nutritionally balanced. Then she would rub the bio-identical hormone creams on my inner thighs, carefully following the instructions on the jars. After approximately 36 hours, I was ready to resume my own care... but it was time for the next surgery.

I had completed the first two surgeries with the endodontist and was now ready to continue on with the periodontist. My reactions to the anesthesia grew increasingly more unpleasant. I had outbursts of anger towards the nurses and even towards Mom and Kevin. I don't recall these at all, but I had glimmers of memory when they were teasing me about them. I must admit that I was a little impressed that I had that in me and could actually be mean!

Nine surgeries later, we were done, but the facial pain had not decreased. In fact, it had become worse, and the search for answers led to a diagnosis of trigeminal neuralgia (TN). The pain was horrible; it felt like someone was stabbing my face and head with little knives, and nothing brought relief. Dr. Buckley and I decided to contact Dr. B, knowing he would have the best recommendations, as he always did.

Email response from Dr. B, dated December 16, 2013

1. Acupuncture can be very helpful for this condition.

2. Gabapentin is a good choice, although to my knowledge, Tegretol (Carbamazepine) is still indicated for TN. Blood levels

need to be drawn to make sure you have no suppression of your white blood cell count. This should help a lot.

3. Mindfulness practices have been shown to be effective (read *Full Catastrophe Living*[11] by Jon Kabat- Zinn).

4. Desensitization... do not hesitate to self-massage and stimulate the area affected. Keeping it sheltered from all stimuli will only make matters worse.

Keep thinking positive thoughts…

Season's Greetings!

Dr. B

I massaged the areas affected as often as I could, but this brought such unbearable pain that it always resulted in violent bouts of vomiting. My heart also pounded so hard it reverberated inside my head. Medications didn't resonate with me, therefore we left that aside and went directly to mindfulness, and I was a pro. I spent the next couple of months meditating four to five times daily and using mindfulness practices at all times. Of course, I had to laugh at my thoughts , they were just so wimpy. I was cracking up all the time on the inside, although you couldn't tell, since I could not smile.

The topic of another surgery once again had to be discussed—a Rhizotomy, which means to partially cut the nerve. This can offer a certain amount of relief, however, it results in the loss of sensation on one side of the face. There are many other potential complications as well, including deafness, numbness and stroke.

After speaking with Dr B and understanding the full picture, this was not something I was interested in whatsoever. I would be drooling for the rest of my life, I would have drooping eyes with a numb face, and hearing loss. It could also result in a stroke. And there was no guarantee that it would have any effect on the pain. I don't think so! My face was already deformed due to all the surgeries; I certainly wasn't going to keep adding to the problem! I had healed my neck with meditation, visualization, and mindfulness using my imagination to move energy. I could certainly heal this.

Diary Entry, May 2, 2014

If I could go back in time and skip the root canal that resulted in trigeminal neuralgia, would I? Would I stop myself from getting on the highway on that cold day in January of 1996? No, I wouldn't. I wouldn't change a single thing. How could I, when it has led to the discovery of what I truly am? This state of Being cannot be adequately described; it must be personally experienced. If awakening has truly occurred, life is so miraculous, abundant and magical. Why would one want to go back?

This Light of consciousness shines ever so brightly. This warm, loving and inviting glow reminds me to be present, and the signposts are everywhere. This light emanates from within me, from the formless dimension within, and has always been there. At first, it was only apparent during meditation, and only for brief moments, but now a constant swirling force of energy circling clockwise inside my torso is continually lighting my way. Words only minimize this; to experience it for yourself is the only way.

An overwhelming passion to help others discover the bliss of Being is my calling. The responsibility to teach those who want to be taught to find their indwelling spirit, or God within, feels like my sole purpose for existence. To help others heal by bringing this consciousness into our world is what I am here to do. Yes, everything is a gift, and I wouldn't change a single thing, even if I could.

Believing that every experience I've had in my life has been absolutely necessary for the evolution of my consciousness has led me to this very moment. True success for me would be to help others discover who they already are. We are essence; we are conscious Beings. There is an alternative to suffering, unhappiness and struggling, and we don't have to be anything other than what we already are. Happiness—true genuine happiness, peace, fulfillment and authentic love is already ours. It always has been because it's already within us. It just needs to be acknowledged and accepted. To help people find that would be true success. *(End of diary entry.)*

Driving back from Ottawa with Kevin after yet another doctor's appointment approximately a month later, I was blinded by a flash of light so bright that I winced and closed my eyes. Slowly opening my eyes again, I realized that I could fully see out of my left eye and the pain had vanished. I screamed, "Oh my God, babe! It's gone and I can see!" He quickly pulled over onto the side of the highway to take me into his arms as we both cried. To feel his lips on mine again, the lips I knew so well, his face against mine, the warmth of his touch... and to once again fully see the beautiful man before me; there are no words. I cried without fearing the pain a tear would produce, and let it all out, after months of holding it in. Kevin held me tightly for what seemed like an eternity; he was always my soft place to fall. It was over. It was really over and I was still here.

When we arrived at the house, I made my way up the stairs as fast as possible and jumped into Mom's lap as she was sitting in her Lazy Boy chair. The anesthesia had taken a toll on my body, and I had lost a lot of weight, but being in Mom's lap again without crushing her... it was all worth it. I tearfully screamed, "Mom it's over! It's really over!" She gasped and gently placed her hand on my cheek. I tilted my head, pushing my face into her loving hand. I knew that hand, every inch of it. She asked if I could see and rejoiced when I told her I could. She took me into her loving embrace and rocked me. We were so blessed.

The light that had been dimmed for almost six months was shining all around me again, emanating from Mom, from Kevin, from everything in the room. The "mini-fireflies" were dancing in delight. Looking up at Mom from beneath my lashes I studied her face—that beautiful face and those beautiful eyes that had so lovingly been with me since the very beginning. We had done it together as a team, and I was here to live this moment. The countless blessings that filled my life, and always had, were impossible to grasp.

The weight loss didn't seem to correlate with the increasing size of my left breast. I didn't think much of it until I was walking out of the bathroom after a shower and Kevin noticed it, saying it was very large with a huge lump on the side of it. I returned to the bathroom to have a look in the mirror and gasped at what I saw. There was a golf-ball sized lump protruding out of the side of my breast. I wasn't too concerned after all the anesthesia medications I'd been given, but Mom put her foot down, and I soon went in to see Dr. Buckley.

Dr. Buckley examined the breast and scheduled an emergency mammogram, as well as an ultrasound. I was at the Winchester Hospital within a couple of days. Everything went well, but due to my ability so see people 's auras and energy, I noticed a shift in the girl performing the ultrasound as she excused herself from the room. She returned informing me that additional images were needed. Afterwards, she ensured me that every possible angle was covered. Then I got dressed and went home. Shortly afterwards, I received a phone call from the nurse. She said there was alarming evidence on the scan, and that she had scheduled an appointment with the oncologist for the following day. She told me that an emergency biopsy had already been ordered. You have got to be kidding me!

Meeting with the oncologist was enlightening, to say the least, but I couldn't help but feel bewildered by the conversation. The doctor said he had 39 "baddies" (as he referred to his patients) last year, and chemo, radiation and mastectomies were all horrific, putting it mildly. He announced that my scans were highly suggestive of malignancy, as he examined the lump and the swelling way into the collar bone. Lying on that bed, I thought about the "39 baddies" and wondered what their names were. I wished so much that I could speak with them, love them and guide them. They weren't "cancers ," they were women. Who was loving them through this? Was I just another cancer sitting before him? No I wasn't. I already knew what I was. But neither were those women, and I so wanted to remind them of what they are.

Considering that I had redefined *pain* by not only changing the sensation, but also my reaction to hearing the word, I could certainly do the same with *cancer*. I immediately began to envision the follow-up appointment with the oncologist , hearing the word *benign*, and enjoying the celebration thereafter, filled with hugs from Kevin and Mom. I expressed my preference by writing in detail about how wonderful this appointment had gone, how utterly elated I was to hear that I was perfectly fine, and how blessed we all were to have received the amazing results.

My breast had doubled in size and the swelling reached up to the collar bone. There were lumps all the way into my armpit. Even the texture of the skin on the breast had changed, and the shape and feel of my nipple was completely different. The symptoms had started on the right side. The oncologist said it didn't look good, but I didn't have to believe him. I stayed positive.

There was no sense in causing myself more suffering by resisting or getting angry. I knew there was a lesson in this, and I had a really good track record for kicking ass and coming out even better. So staying focused on gratitude for the amazing blessings in my life was priority number one—without judgment of this situation. Mom and Kevin were worried, but I kept them laughing by flashing my extremely large breasts and giggling at how bouncy they were as I jumped up and down.

Two people played a crucial role in my life at this time and inspired me beyond belief—Angel Girard Forget and her son Chad Girard. They had both been diagnosed with cancer and were going through treatment at the same time. I couldn't wrap my head around this. The Facebook page they had created in support of Chad always brought tears to my eyes. Regardless of how difficult it got, regardless of the setbacks they were facing, their page was always filled with inspiration as they celebrated their blessings. They were both going through severe ordeals, yet here they were inspiring others, including me. Not once did they complain about their situation. Their sole focus was to bring light to a dark subject and they excelled at it. Mother and son conquered cancer together.

This was the outcome, as I knew it would be. Their journey had been one of acceptance, gratitude and love.

Email correspondence between Dr. B and me, dated June 29, 2014

Hi Dr. B, how are you? I am elated, totally. I DON'T have breast cancer! After seeing the scary news from the scans and meeting with the specialist to discuss options, I decided (not surprisingly) to take this into my own hands. I had three weeks before my biopsy, and knew I could turn things around. I meditated four to five times a day, did a healing body scan prior to sleep, constantly sent healing energy to my breast, and used mindfulness practices. I repeated the positive affirmation "I am perfect health" faithfully. I also used a very special essential oil called Transformation™ by Young Living™ to help change negative emotions. This oil contains idaho blue spruce, palo santo, ocotea and frankincense.

The day of the biopsy, the first doctor couldn't find anything on the ultrasound, and she had a very confused look on her face. The second doctor came in and had the same look. They did do the biopsy, but they had to use the previous scans because the cancer was gone. They were completely baffled. I thought to myself, "If you only knew what I've been able to do in the past to heal myself..." and giggled. Later, I met with the oncologist, and he too, was quite confused. I felt him out a little asking if he believed in meditation, mindfulness, self-healing, etc., but he wasn't receptive. Still, I told him what I had done and got the familiar "you're whacked" face. But that's just fine with me.

Anyway, thought I'd let you know the great news. If only everyone knew how powerful they were!

Sincerely, Tina xo

Response from Dr B:

Tina!

Thanks for sharing this wonderful story with me! I am absolutely convinced of the body-mind's ability to heal itself! You are an inspiration; keep in touch!

Regards,
Dr. B

Diary Entry, July 2, 2014

Some have labelled the last few months of my life as "tragic" or "unfair" or "heartbreaking." Those are the most popular reactions. "Is this ever going to end for her? Hasn't she had enough? Her poor husband and mom... how can they bear this?" Not even close! "Pure bliss" is much more accurate! The greatest gifts come through the toughest of times, and this I know for sure—I am the blessed one.

I've been debating telling everyone the whole story, since the reactions I get to just a glimpse of this are usually, "Oh my God, you've been dealing with all of this, but you're still writing about love and ecstatic happiness all over Facebook! How is this possible?" Or, "You've got to be kidding me. You've been going through all of these horrendous surgeries, yet helping me with my measly problems?"

It's funny really, because I am so very blessed, so very grateful for my journey and everything it consists of. I wouldn't be who I am if one single thing was different, and for that, I would do it all again. My label for everything is "pure love," because it is! And it just keeps magnifying and expanding. I see beauty, love and light in absolutely everything, and I am constantly fascinated. Nothing happens *to* you, it all happens *for* you. Don't struggle, just love. Don't fret, just love. Don't feel sorry for yourself or others, just love. Don't let fear dictate your perceptions and beliefs, just love. Don't let judgmental thoughts cloud your vision, just love.

Don't allow anything to interfere with love, it is the most powerful source of energy we have... and the most valuable. It changes you. It changes everything. Cherish and protect it. Everyone is free to feel love, it's a simple choice and it truly does change everything. Choose only your preference and let go of the rest. If happiness is your preference, then choose happiness. If love is your preference, then choose love. If awe is your preference, then choose awe. There is no universal Law of Lack, there is only a Law of Abundance. And abundance is what you are. It's that simple. If I can make such a bold statement, anyone can.

My inner purpose is my outer purpose. The only time that truly exists is the present moment, now, and it already is as it is. So what can I bring to it, other than complete acceptance, non-resistance and non-judgment? Past and future are only part of our thoughts. By being awakened and aware, you realize that you are the space behind your thoughts and not the thoughts themselves. Therefore, thoughts no longer provoke unwanted emotions or reactions. What happens or doesn't happen no longer determines my happiness or unhappiness, since true happiness emanates from within me. If negative emotions arise, I know that my thoughts are off track and have no basis in reality. So I go within, witness my thoughts, and usually have a good laugh.

Even upon hearing the word *cancer*, I remained the loving witness and chose to maintain my vibration with laughter and joy. The outcome was the one I anticipated. I believed to my core that I was perfect health, and although thoughts of doubt and fear arose, I remained steadfast. I did not waste one moment feeling sad, dejected or afraid. Through meditation, loving myself uncondi-tionally and choosing what I wanted (choosing what excited me the most) and following it without fail, I already knew I was fine. This is the gift of knowing your true power! I am so immensely grateful for my journey, every single moment of it.

This ever-present peaceful stillness inside me determines my thoughts, actions and steps. It always comes from a place within, filled with a deep sense of love, peace and acceptance—it is my very Being. This energy, this Life that I now know myself to be, and recognize every human being to be... is love, pure love. Helping others to make the same discovery is my only true purpose. This is how I feel with every fiber of my Being, and this will come to be. The Universe and God will call on me. Until then, I can share my love, energy and peace with anyone and everyone who wants it and needs it. It is only mine to give, and I give it freely. All will see their purpose in my glowing face and my love-filled eyes; they will hear Spirit calling them in my blissful laugh. *(End of diary entry.)*

PART THREE - JUST HERE!

CHAPTER SIXTEEN
Blue Skies, Blue Eyes

Mom had been to visit her cousin not far from where we lived and upon her return, Kevin and I could feel her excitement. She began by reminding me of his daughter's wedding we had attended many years ago, and asked if I remembered what I told her during the ceremony. I fondly recalled the little village where the wedding had taken place and the beautiful stained glass windows of the chapel. Then it came back to me, what I had whispered to Mom during the ceremony: "Wouldn't this be the most beautiful place to live, Mom? The energy is breathtaking!"

Mom laughed and couldn't wait to tell us that the wedding had taken place exactly where we were living, in the small village of Williamsburg, and that Kevin and I had been married in the exact same chapel. I was speechless! It had been obvious the moment we drove by this subdivision four-years prior that this was where we were going to live. The energy had been familiar and exhilarating, and I was not going to ignore this signpost, regardless of the flack I took. Sitting in that chapel all those years ago, I had planted the seed and it had blossomed magnificently. We were living in the exact same place I had dreamed of years ago, yet I had not even the slightest clue; I thought I had found it totally by "accident." How miraculous!

Danielle had passed away on August 14th, 2012. The two-year anniversary was soon approaching, and an inspiration to go sky-diving suddenly hit me. This had been on my "bucket list" since my teens. Believing as we all do, that I had time, I put it on the back burner to pursue my education and career. The accident happened not long afterwards. This was a long time coming, and I couldn't have been more excited as I announced on Facebook that I was going skydiving! I remembered clearly what I had asked Danielle to promise me that day in the hospital, so I picked the day following the two-year mark, which was August 15th, 2014.

To my complete dismay, Kevin was furious. He angrily told me, "You've had nine surgeries in the past year alone, and I've almost lost you how many times? And now you 're going to jump out of a plane?" He didn't speak to me for two days, and I was just as pissed off, so I wasn't talking to him either. Mom broke the ice and lovingly said to Kevin, "Ya know Kevin, we need to have faith in Tina, to believe in her. She's gotten herself through the unthinkable; she has survived what should have killed her. This makes me nervous too, but I trust my daughter. She has certainly proven herself. This is something she needs to do; there is something waiting for her up there, and you surely don't want to be the one standing in her way. You know she won't do this without your blessing, as she would never hurt you. You need to be there with her as she finally gets to experience this." I was so grateful and filled with so much love for her. She knew me to the depths of my core, and after everything she'd witnessed, her faith was unshakeable.

I sent Dr. B an email asking what he thought of this idea, and of course he was 100% supportive, encouraging me to live this dream. This was his response:

Hello Tina,

Having done such a tandem "parasail" jump myself, I can only attest to how smooth the landing was (in very wind-still conditions). Obviously, one cannot predict changes in the wind patterns, but all things being equal, and if you choose the day properly for your jump , I see absolutely no reason not to.

Kind Regards and Good Luck,
Dr. B

After seeing the email response from Dr. B, and after a long conversation in which I explained in detail the preparations made with the special tandem partner, Kevin was fully and enthusiastically onboard. I was so blessed! How I adored him. I fell in love with him all over again for standing by me and making yet another dream come true, even though he didn't agree with it in the slightest. If he had known what I had asked Danielle before she passed, this would not be happening, so I was beyond thankful that I had kept that to myself.

My sister-in-law Darlene, my niece Kayla, and her friend Stephanie, decided to skydive with me. The weekend soon arrived. Kathleen, my stepdaughter, was visiting from Alberta. I was so happy she was here to live this dream with me, as we had become the best of friends over the years. My sister-in-law Joyce, her husband Mike, and my brother-in-law Rick, Darlene's husband, came down to watch this magnificent dream come true, and I couldn't have loved them more for doing so.

Our jump was scheduled for 10:00 a.m. on Saturday, August 15th, 2014. That morning, the phone rang and it was ParachuteGoSkydiving,™ informing us that the jump was cancelled due to weather conditions. This was not happening! I asked the girl to reschedule us for the next day, but they were fully booked. I explained that my family had driven nine hours for this and that we would really appreciate if she could somehow squeeze us in for a jump. She asked me to give her some time and she would see what she could do. There was no doubt in my mind—we were going to jump. The phone rang again a couple of hours later, and it was the same girl whom I had spoken with earlier. She announced that some regulars had given up their slots for us, and that our jump was scheduled for 10:00 a.m. on Sunday, August 16th, 2014. We were beyond excited and couldn't wait for morning to come.

It was a long walk to the portable for check-in, but Kevin assisted me all the way and carried my bags along with the special pillow I needed in order to be able to sit. Holding his hand and knowing he supported this dream meant everything to me; it would not have happened otherwise. As we checked-in, filled out the forms and were weighed, I couldn't contain my excitement. I just couldn't believe I was finally doing this!

The weather still wasn't cooperating, so we were sent to a large tent where the instructors were hanging out. That's where I got to meet Stephane, my tandem partner. Over the next couple of hours, I filled him in as much as I could on what had transpired over the last eighteen years. He was blown away, and he couldn't wait to make this dream come true for me. Stephane explained how he would take the landing for me to prevent any impact to my body. With the biggest smile on his face, he expressed that he was grateful that he was going to experience this with me.

Our group was finally called to suit up; it was our turn. I couldn't wait to get to the dressing tent; I was so excited that I felt like I was going to burst. Once we were all suited up and about to make our way to the plane, we heard "weather delay" over the loud speaker. Everyone's faces fell. For the next three hours, I must have heard that we were never going to skydive today and that there was no sign of clearing in the skies a dozen times. But there was absolutely no doubt in me. I kept repeating to myself, "Danielle just needs more time; she's setting something up and wants it to be perfect. I know she's pulling strings with God. We are definitely jumping today." Danielle never got the chance to skydive, but she was skydiving today, since I had some of her ashes tucked in a little container in my suit.

The afternoon seemed to drag on, but my elation didn't waver in the least. At approximately 4:00 p.m. we heard our group being called over the loud speaker once again, so we proceeded to go and suit up. Putting on the blue suit, followed by the harness, I knew we were jumping this time. I was filled with so much bliss that my cheeks hurt from all the smiling.

A man I hadn't seen before appeared before me to help me suit up. He announced that he was Moe, my tandem partner. Where was Stephane? I saw Kevin's face fall, but I flashed the biggest smile at him. I knew this was all fate; it was all part of the plan. I hugged Kevin, Mom and Kathleen before heading to the buggy for transportation to the plane. I grabbed Kathleen's hand to bring her along for the ride. Joyce jumped on as well, just to capture on video our excitement on the way to the plane. This was it! This was really it!

I must have been rushing to the plane because I felt my tandem partner's hand reach out for mine to slow me down. He leaned me back against him, quickly explaining what I needed to do, but I didn't hear a thing. As he lifted my head back against his shoulder, I caught a glimpse of the sky and smiled as the thought of Danielle filled me with pure love. The door of the plane was open and everyone piled in. I wanted to jump first, so Moe and I got in last.

As the door to the small aircraft closed, it dawned on me that I should probably fill Moe in on my injuries. I quickly ticked off what I had been through, and his reaction was priceless. He leaned closer for me so I could hear him over the loud engine and proceeded to tell me that I had nothing to worry about. He had experienced something similar and was not supposed to survive. When the doctors told him he would never walk again, his reply was that he would not only walk, he would fly. We both broke into a joyous laughter realizing that it was indeed fate that we met. As we reached higher altitudes I asked my second jumper with the GoPro™ helmet to take a video as I talked to Danielle: "Danielle, I know you never got a chance to do this for real, but you're doing this with me. I love you."

Above the clouds, I looked out the window and was filled with awe. I was here to live this moment. Tears streamed down my face. The sights, the day's events, and even the perfect timing was not lost on me. This was miraculous. The door opened and we were ready and lined up. It was time. The force of the wind took me by surprise as I placed my foot on the bar outside the plane, but the video clearly shows that the smile never left my face. Moe grabbed my head leaning it back onto his shoulder, and yelled, "One, two, three, go!" We barrel-rolled out of the aircraft and into a free fall.

I had no access to thought or emotion; the sensations were too overwhelming as we plummeted from the sky. I felt Moe pull my hands off my harness, spreading them to each side to fly. I cannot find the words to express what I was feeling; even "pure love" doesn't come close.

A familiar voice saying, "*I have always had you, I always will. I will never let you go...*" penetrated every cell of my body. It was God. A huge white orb appeared in front of me with a smaller one by its side, along with a trillion of the purest diamonds, all reflecting the colors off each other in the most brilliant light. They were fractals of light, and they were all moving in unison in the grandest of designs, some to the right and some to the left. They were all inside of each other in swirling motions. It was the most breathtaking performance in existence, like the most glorious of starling murmurations, each in their own colors. The orbs were moving through the fractals like fish through water with the light separating, wrapping around them, then rejoining in perfect harmony.

I caught sight of my hands, and my skin looked just like the fractals. It felt like I was in the palm of God's hand and He was giving me a tour, with Danielle right beside me. She looked as I remembered her, with her piercing blue eyes and her stunning smile. I kissed her as tears streamed down my face. But they weren't tears of sadness, they were tears of awe, because I now knew exactly where she was and how ecstatically blissed out she was. I was so overwhelmingly happy for her that my heart felt like it would burst out of my chest. "Overjoyed, elated, and in ecstasy" doesn't even begin to describe what heaven felt like. Her only request was that I speak with my godparents, her mom and dad, to tell them all about where she was.

The feeling of heaven... there truly are no words; one must experience this state for themselves to have any inkling, for it is not of this world. I can give you a glimpse, but it's just a glimpse. Imagine the most toe-curling, back-arching, thought-annihilating, mind-blowing orgasm you've ever had—the kind where tears spring to your eyes as you reach the climax. And multiply that by infinity. Now imagine that this state is never diminished in the slightest, the sensation never stops, and you'll get a glimpse of what heaven feels like. The completeness of the connection, being plugged in with Source, with God, is beyond anything we could ever experience here on Earth. It's not simply that negativity, darkness and heartbreak don't exist; it's that there is absolutely no memory, awareness or experience of it. It is pure bliss. It is pure awe. It is pure, unconditional, unwavering and unending love. The only physical comparison I can make to the feeling of heaven is the orgasm.

Upon landing, I truly couldn't process what had happened; I was stunned and bewildered. I have no memory of what was said or done after landing, but it was caught on video by Kevin. The words, "I went to heaven and I didn't even have to die," came out of my mouth, which couldn't have been more accurate. I was certainly in heaven but did I die? I had no idea. I hugged Darlene. It would take weeks to process everything that had happened, but instantly I realized something was drastically different. I had no pain and my body was foreign to me.

On the ride home I tried to tell Kevin, but I was at a loss for words. A miracle had taken place. I would repeatedly turn to him with wide eyes and say, "Oh my God, babe!" but nothing else would come out. There was something else that was very foreign to me—I was hungry for real food and couldn't wait to dig into some vegetables, fries, potatoes, or whatever else I could get my hands on. It had been eleven years since I'd eaten solid food, how was this possible? The entire ride home I felt absolutely no pain. I threw my special pillow in the back seat, knowing I no longer needed it or any of the medical equipment and aids. How was this possible?

I was walking, running, eating, loving and literally bouncing off the walls test-driving this new body to the fullest. I had an abundance of energy and just couldn't sit still. I wanted to taste every aspect of the life that had eluded me for eighteen years. Kevin and Mom watched me in complete disbelief, not knowing what to say or do. They were in shock as well, watching me bounce and dance around the house unassisted. They would tell me every once in a while to calm down, to slow down because they didn't want me overdoing it and getting sick again. But this was just asking the impossible.

I couldn't contain myself. I was cooking, cleaning, eating and doing everything else that a typical person took for granted, and I was delighting in all of it. Mom went to spend time with her brother, my Uncle Joe, and I spent my days dancing as I cooked beautiful meals for my husband. I dressed up the table, which I could now sit at, with candles, hearts and anything else I could think of. I was awaiting him at the door when he got home from work in the most beautiful lingerie. I was pain-free and living life to the fullest, excited by everything.

It was time to check out the Parachute Go Skydive™ USB stick. I placed it into the port of my computer, anxiously wanting to watch the jump itself. I discovered there were approximately 400 images captured that day, and I began looking at them one by one. I must have looked at those images a dozen times, but couldn't stop myself from going through them again and again. The orbs that I had seen were captured, as well as the most beautiful rainbow. There were also images of me kissing with tears streaming down my face. I knew who I was kissing in those images.

Kevin sat beside me to look through the images when he suddenly asked me to pause the image that was on the screen. He told me to look at my eyes in the picture. They were blue. My eyes are dark brown, and not even close to blue, but there they were, as light blue as the sky. I couldn't believe what I was seeing. Why were they blue? There were approximately twenty images where my eyes were blue, but I had no understanding as to why. I knew I had been to heaven, I knew my body was healed, but why were my eyes a piercing blue? My eye color never changed back to dark brown after this. To this day, my eyes are blue/green.

I had told my friend Lisa all about my trip to heaven. I wanted her to see the images that had been captured, so I headed to her place. We sat on her back deck as I opened iPhoto on my laptop, and without thought, also took out Danielle's obituary so she would know who I was talking about when I said that I saw Danielle.

Her jaw dropped as she saw Danielle's blue eyes. She blurted out, "Tina, you have Danielle 's eyes!" I grabbed the obituary while scrutinizing the pictures of me and burst into tears. Those were Danielle's eyes in the pictures! I knew I would see her the day of the skydive, and she, along with God, had given me this miracle. After noticing Danielle's date of birth, Lisa mentioned that she was born two days after that. She then asked what time Danielle passed away, as well as what time I had jumped out of the plane. I had no idea, but I was going to find out.

I rushed home to put the USB stick back into the computer and saw that the jump was between 4:42 and 4:46 p.m. This was the same time at which the respiratory therapist walked into that hospital room to turn off Danielle's CPAP on August 14, 2012. My skydive was on August 16th, but the time was exact. I was speechless and in a dream-like state, everything seemed surreal. Had Danielle's soul stepped into my body to show me what heaven was like, and hence the blue eyes? Or had I died? I would never know the answer to this question but I didn't care. I had to get to Uncle Danny and Aunt Sue and tell them the truth of what happened that day. I had to tell them where Danielle was, and that I saw her. I had to show them these pictures!

Packing for the trip with Kevin, I fell to my knees. I was sobbing with my face buried in my hands upon noticing the three empty suitcases on the floor. The realization was finally hitting me. I yelled out, "It's over, babe, it's really over! Look at the empty suitcases that used to carry all my medical stuff! Only one suitcase for the two of us, babe. We can go wherever we want to now, and we don't have to panic about forgetting something or lugging five suitcases around. It's over, babe. I'm finally free."

The poor prognoses and the zero-chance of recovery were bull-shit. My pre-accident abilities were mine once again! This was truly foreign to me, it had been so long. Kevin picked me up and took me into his loving arms as I cried, finally comprehending the magnitude of this miracle.

Arriving in the little town seven hours away, I poked at my right leg, hip and lower back, still astonished by their complete lack of protest. We parked in front of the motel and Kevin jumped out to carry everything in, as I thoughtlessly swung a bag over my shoulder.

I couldn't help but giggle loudly as we made our way into the room. This new body was outstanding! It was late and we were tired, but so deliriously happy.

It was approximately 4:00 a.m. when I woke Kevin up. I was feeling really weird. I kept repeating that I felt really weird, and he was ready to call 911. He asked me to explain what I was feeling, but I was embarrassed and had no idea how to explain this other than as weird. "There's a weird pressure in my bum and it's really uncomfortable!" I finally blurted out. He suggested that maybe I needed to have a bowel movement, but that was impossible—it had been thirteen years since I'd had the urge.

He got out of bed, took my hand and walked me to the bathroom. He told me to sit on the toilet and relax as he shut the door. Okay, now I was in shock. What on earth do I do? There was no way that was going down the toilet, and how does this even work? It had been thirteen years since I'd felt the sensations one feels when they need to have a bowel movement. I had no clue what was happening nor had I even remembered what a stool looked like, as it was all taken care of for me and everything that was done was out of sight.

Again, completely embarrassed, I came out of the bathroom and while looking at my husband, I pointed to the toilet saying, "Okay, now what? What do I do with that, babe? There's no way a poop like that can just be flushed down the toilet. Do I put it into in a bag?" Laughing at my innocence, he walked to the toilet and flushed it, as I watched in total amazement. I actually went to the bathroom by myself... well kind of. My loving husband had guided me through this process, which was very new to me. But I did have the bowel movement on my own. It was really over!

The second Kevin and I arrived at my uncle's, I jumped out of the truck. I threw my purse to the ground and leaped into my Uncle Marcel's arms, wrapping my legs around his waist as he laughed wholeheartedly. As Mom pulled up behind us, I made my way to Danielle's mom and dad, taking them both into my arms as I sobbed. "I saw Danielle, Uncle Danny! I saw Danielle, Aunt Sue! And if you could see where she is, you would be so happy. She's so happy, Uncle Danny! She's so happy, Aunt Sue! You would never cry again if you could see how happy she is. She's free and she's so happy." We held each other for a long time, until we could finally stop crying.

I took my laptop out of the case to show them the images that had been captured, as they watched in disbelief. I told them what really happened the day Danielle died, and they said they had been wondering about it for a long time now. The fact that her body was already in rigor mortis when her death was announced hadn't made any sense at all. I could finally breathe a sigh of relief—they knew the truth and they weren't angry at all. In fact, they were happy I had been there with Danielle in her final moments.

Uncle Marcel grabbed my hand to show me a computer program called Trinfinity8[12] he was using for healing. Upon seeing the computer screen I gasped. This was exactly what I saw in heaven: the fractals, the colors, the light, the movement, the motions. I told him that is what I saw as I pointed to his computer screen. He said I was lucky to be here; that having been that far into heaven I should have landed to the ground dead. So I must have chosen to come back, although I didn't remember being given a choice. I was in heaven, I heard God's voice, I loved on Danielle, then I was back. During those three minutes or so, I felt like I had never had an earthly existence and that I had always been snug as a bug in a rug in heaven. I recall my lifeless body hanging in the harness once I was back from heaven, and my inability to move, but I had no idea what really happened. And to this day, I don't know. Either I died during the skydive or Danielle's soul stepped into my body to show me where she was and what it was like.

Uncle Marcel announced that we were heading over to Andre's for a family get together, so we made our way over. I couldn't wait to give my cousin Andre the biggest hug. The food was beautifully displayed and filled the entire table. It caught my attention; I was starving! I filled my plate and mindlessly threw morsels of various foods into my mouth, savoring every favor. I walked out to grab a seat on the deck. As I started eating, a silence fell as everyone watched with their mouths open, unable to believe what they were seeing—I was eating. Their surprise was obvious, yet I couldn't stop devouring the glorious food on my plate. I even stole a little piece of chicken and sausage, though I had been a vegetarian for over twenty years.

Andre and his friend started playing guitar, and everyone joined in to sing some of our favorite country songs. I just had to dance, and I grabbed Uncle Marcel's hand. We waltzed our waltz as we had done all those years ago, picking up right where we left off. I then showed off a very cool line dance, and I caught my Aunt Sue shaking her head from side to side in utter disbelief as she looked over at Mom. Yes, this was real. And it was shocking to say the least.

It was as if the accident had never happened and the last eighteen years had been wiped clean. My dream of a capable pain-free body was a reality; it had really come true. There had been countless doubts, obstacles and challenges along the way, but the vision of my dream remained strong. I had a new body, a new reality and a new life. The promise I had asked of Danielle she had indeed kept—she had brought me to heaven with her. But I got to return. I saw through her eyes what awaits us all, and I experienced a love that is beyond words.

Although I didn't remember being given a choice to return, I knew exactly the reason I had returned. My purpose, my calling, my mission was to bring heaven to earth; for people to discover heaven on earth. Looking into my family's eyes, or even into the eyes of a person passing me on the street, there was a spark of recognition and I was in heaven all over again. A realization washed over me—we don't need to become anything at all; we are already perfect and whole. The only limitations we have are those we put upon ourselves. Life is an illusion, a game, and it cannot be won, it can only be played. We need to release everything we are not, which life put upon us, and shed it freely without labels. We need to say Yes to this destruction and allow what we've always been to rise from the ashes. We already are pure Divine Love; we just need to release the shadows to reveal the Self.

Epilogue

You are so confident in faithfully following the signposts on every street corner to reach your destination, yet you are skeptical and unsure with the most important signposts of all. Emotions, illness, occurrences, accidents, happiness and excitement are all signposts, and if you learn to trust them without interpretation, the state of being and destination you desire is just as certain. Drop all beliefs, opinions, judgments and biases. Then look inward, look outward, and what is left is the truth. By removing the filter of pre-conceived notions, the truth will reveal itself and you will remember what you are and always have been.

I had a deep sense of gratitude for my journey, however, I still had some questions. I fully realized long ago that I was indeed creating my reality, but the fact that I continued to manifest health challenges when I was unshakeable in my commitment and focus on my desired feeling of joy, was baffling to me. This became clear when my best friend sent me the following, written by Bentinho Massaro.

"At first, spirituality is all about the individual waking up to the deeper layers of their consciousness, and integrating these truths—both the transcendental truths as well as the hidden, suppressed personal beliefs—until one comes into unison within one's self. Then, spirituality becomes all about being of service to other-selves, who are all portions of the over-arching being that you/I/we are.

When most of the personal doubts and separations have been resolved, there is no greater honor for the individual than to be so fully of service that he sees nothing but the One Infnite Creator interacting with itself in infinite ways through endless individuations. This state cannot be explained nor understood until experienced first-hand, but there is no greater satisfaction than to be of service to the All.

In fact, after one has gone through most of one's own spiritual growth, the only way to evolve even further is to direct that spiritual awareness unto the rest of one's Self (aka other-selves) and commit to that so fully that one becomes even more self-transcendent in their consciousness.

There is no way to describe this state of being as it is truly trans-personal. The balance of love, wisdom, confidence, tact and humility that one gets to learn in these rapturous (as well as heart-breaking) scenarios, which the soul then attracts to its personality-extensions, is so subtle that no teaching except the living of it can touch upon this reality.

Make no mistake, this is the state I prepare you all for in my Trinfnity Academy™13 and through my teachings. I might talk about attracting your dream life, and you will be able to manifest that too, using these tools, but it will also naturally evolve you into a "shepherding consciousness" to which I cannot speak in words, except barely. But when that stage has fully arrived for you, we will be able to look each other in the eyes when we meet and share instant tears of gratitude and ungraspable recognition of each other's beingness, fearless heart and journey. We will see the oneness of our vision and purpose. There is no greater joy, no deeper honor, than to be of service to others in the most intangible of ways.

May you know your utter union with the Creator through all experience and catalyst that you attract to yourself as a human today. We will meet as brothers and sisters of light when the time comes for you to have passed successfully through the challenge of loneliness and misunderstanding.

The ultimate reward lies on the other side of your unconditional willingness to give ever more of yourself to those who ask for your soul to be present here on earth.

I love you more than you know."

I was speechless! He had not only summed up my 21-year journey, he had also described the absolute sense of oneness I was experiencing since being in heaven, seeing Source in everyone I come across. When my best friend Lisanne and I first met, we ran into each other's arms, sobbing in recognition of one another, even though we had never met and had only exchanged messages over social media. We loved each other fully and completely and felt that we had known each other for a thousand years. She was the one who sent me Bentinho's post.

"We will be able to look each other in the eyes when we meet and share instant tears of gratitude and ungraspable recognition of each other's beingness, fearless heart and journey. We will see the oneness of our vision and purpose. There is no greater joy, no deeper honor, than to be of service to others in the most intangible of ways." (Bentinho Massaro)

I knew instantly this recognition would occur with Bentinho, that he knew the truth, the absolute truth, and that heaven could certainly be experienced while living, since this was within us all.

Bentinho Massaro is only 31 years old as of this writing; how does he know all of this? The urge to discover his teachings was undeniable. I soon began watching his videos on YouTube and I signed up for his online Enlightenment and Empowerment classes[14]. There I discovered yet another signpost, the name of his academy, Trinfinity. This had been the program my Uncle Marcel had been using for healing, Trinfinity8, which had the computer graphics that portrayed exactly what I had seen in heaven. This was meant to be!

Upon playing the first video, I was awe-struck, for all I could see was a purple and indigo aura with a very distorted background. I could not see him at all. I've had the ability to see auras and energy since I was a child, but I had never experienced this before. Assuming it was a computer glitch, I proceeded to the next video, but it was the same. He was completely transparent to me. It struck me that he had truly transcended the physical form and that I was recognizing this in him, as well as in myself. I watched every video of his available and completed his online classes, which answered the many questions that had been eluding me.

Then I noticed that he was holding an event in none other than Sedona, Arizona... another signpost. My promise to Danielle to release her ashes at the top of Bell Rock was about to be fulfilled and I was finally going to meet Bentinho Massaro. How poetic. How I hoped I'd be able to see him face-to-face!

I only caught a glimpse of his physical form for a brief moment when he walked onto the stage, but I was looking at an empty chair on stage. Why couldn't I see him? As if I was going to spend five days looking at a chair! I was staying at an AirBnb and my housemates Marie, Patricia, Arjen and Jahnavi were fully aware of what was happening. They kept asking if I could see him, but I couldn't. I did notice something different, however. The energy emanating from Bentinho was huge, the sphere almost taking up the entire stage, while in all the videos I had seen, his energy was closer to his body.

At the first invite onto the stage, I raised my hand, not even hearing the question he had asked, which in hindsight, makes me giggle. As I looked into his eyes I saw Source, I saw Truth. There was an instant and ungraspable recognition of each other's beingness, fearless heart and journey. It literally took my breath away. We hugged each other for what seemed like an eternity, becoming one being and the entire Universe at the same time. I am eternally grateful for Bentinho Massaro, my brother, for putting all the pieces of the puzzle together for me and for countless others.

That five-day retreat broke me wide open and answered the last of my questions. The collective energy of this community was unlike anything I had experienced before. It was freedom, acceptance, non-judgment, limitlessness and pure love. To share space with "others," yet truly feel as One, is beyond description. It must be experienced to understand, but this was indeed the state of Oneness shared by all of us. I also discovered that health challenges had been my "theme" and the path on which I had chosen to learn and grow. Obviously, it had been very effective. This allowed me to accept my path, to realize that I was truly limitless, and to release my theme, as it was no longer necessary for the evolution of my consciousness.

My theme was extreme to say the least, but the destination I so desired had been reached by learning to read the signposts and having unwavering faith as I followed them. Any negative emotion was a clear signal that what I was thinking in that moment had no basis in reality, therefore it was dropped with an instant return to love. My sole focus became maintaining the feeling I desired, no matter what, and this I achieved even in extreme circumstances. This proved beyond a shadow of a doubt that circumstances have absolutely no effect on your state of being.

Bentinho's teachings brought every experience and discovery along the way to a beautiful conclusion, by explaining in vivid detail everything I had gone through and why I was still here. The state of being he speaks of I had experienced in heaven, but this state was brought back with me and awaits us all. It already exists, always has and always will, you just have to step into it.

The answers had always already been inside of me and that's why I could never find what I was looking for; I had been searching, seeking everywhere but within. Burdened with low self-esteem, being judgmental, critical, overly sensitive and argumentative—why had I become like this? I kept looking to my childhood, issues with my family, past sexual abuse, the accident... these were all external factors and thoughts. They were my story, which is not who I am, and have never been. This more complete sense of self that I'd been longing for, my Being, had always already been here, but it had been obscured by thoughts of my story, memories and things.

This light has been lit inside and I can see. I can touch Love in all of its fullness and aliveness. I can drink Life in all of its beauty and sacredness. I can feel Energy in all of its sensations and frequencies. I can smell Peace in all of its fragrance and serenity. And in this very moment, I Am One with all of them.

Negativity, hatred, and darkness are all the same energy. You cannot fight against it with the same energy; it's a losing battle. Nor can you judge this energy and expect to have any desired effect over it. Turn on the love, the light, and you can overcome anything. What do you do when you walk into a dark room? You flick on the light and the darkness evaporates. Let your light shine so brightly that others can see their way out of the dark. The only perpetrator of evil in this universe is unconsciousness. It's not personal, it just is. You are Presence, you are Love, you are Consciousness... look within.

This has been a journey and you've traveled it with me, growing every step of the way. Know that everything I said to "Marie" at the end of every chapter I was also saying to you. Take my hand, remember what you are and let's walk into the light together. As I am sitting here writing this, tears stream down my face in joyous celebration of our love-filled reunion. I await your arrival.

Facebook Post, October 15, 2019

A huge epiphany hit me like a ton of bricks a few days ago and I'm finally ready to share.

I've been unfair with many of you by telling you that if you don't like who you are and what's haunting you, then just drop it. It's simple and it's easy, and if it was truly what you wanted, you would have done it by now.

I understand now. I didn't before.

When you're told you are out out of time by a doctor, you change. Everything changes instantly. Whether you have one year, six months, a month or two weeks is irrelevant. You now know the meaning of time.

Any patterns and/or distortions immediately vanish. The drama you create for yourself and others is simply no longer part of you, and you certainly wouldn't waste one precious moment or breath with anything meaningless.

Resentment, anger, frustration, annoyance, judgment, fear, worry and bitterness disappear without a trace. There is only love for yourself, for your loved ones and for the so-called "strangers" who cross your path. It's a love you haven't experienced—trust me. This state must be experienced to be understood.

All of your moments are filled to the brim with laughter, a giving heart and an overflowing soul that makes tears stream down your face. You are in awe of the beauty around you that had eluded you for so long. You immediately get it. You are instantly awakened.

There is no downloading, integrating, shadow work, therapy, days in distress, etc. It is automatic and instantaneous. You don't remember the person you were and you honestly believe that this is you—because it is. This is you and always has been, but you've chosen to cover it all up for some reason. You are convinced that it is difficult and requires much time and effort to just be you.

This is certainly proof that stripping away all of life's layers and returning to what you've always been is not hard. It is not work. It is a given when it "really counts."

When you are told you are out of time, you don't start reading spiritual books, seeking for spiritual teachers, attending retreats and/or begging for guidance from coaches to help you discover enlightenment. It is done with no effort on your part.

I have been told by doctors countless times that I'm dying, to the point where I felt invincible. However, I recently ran out of time while I was in Panama. My heart stopped. I was gone.

I'm back, and my doctors are on it, so don't fret. I'm fine. I won't go into details, but let me say that I don't think my husband, Kevin Blackwell, will ever be the same. Had it not been for this man, I would not be here. Although he thought he didn't know what to do, he did exactly what was required of him. He brought me back. His cry, his love, brought me back.

Kent MacLeod is on it. NutriChem Compounding Pharmacy and Clinic is on it. Dr. Buckley is on it. Dr. B is on it. My body is slowly coming back on board; it's just going to take a bit of time. And unlike every other time my life was on the line, I am not picking up my boxing gloves to fight my way back. I am surrendering. And it is miraculous, to say the least.

This brought me to the epiphany: I've had this advantage over all of you. I know how fleeting life is. I have died more than once but came back to spread this message; to complete my mission.

I wish that each and every one of you would be told by a doctor that you are out of time, and then have the chance to really live. We would have a very different world. But I'm dreaming in color.

Please use my example and truly put yourself in my shoes. Visualize yourself sitting in front of a doctor as he or she tells you that you are out of time. Feel this!

What would you do differently? Who would you be? What have you left undone?

I am telling you that you are out of time! You can experience this state of being if you are willing to lose everything that you are not. You can take these words and let them instantaneously transform and shift you. Or you can continue as you are.

Either way, I will love you. And there's nothing you can do about that.

Endnotes

1   Rhonda Byrne, The Secret, (Pennsylvania: Simon & Schuster, 2006)

2   James Redfield, Celestine Prophecy, (USA: Warner Brothers, 1993)

3   Eckhart Tolle, A New Earth, (USA, Penguin, 2005)

4   Ibid page 37

5   Jessi Alexander and John Mabe, The Climb, Miley Cyrus, The Time of Our Lives, March 5, 2009, Walt Disney Records, Released and created for Hannah Montana: The movie

6   Johnny Kirkland Reid and Thomas Ronald Hardwell, Thank You, performed by Johnny Reid on Kicking Stones, April 10, 2007, Label: Open Road

7   NutriChem Compounding Pharmacy and Clinic, 2599 Carling Avenue, Ottawa, ON Canada, www.nutrichem.com

8   Ibid

[9] Ibid

[10] Richard Marx, This I Promise You, NSYNC, Days In Avalon, October 27, 2000 video debut, Richard Marx, November 2000

[11] John Kabat-Zinn, PhD., Full Catastrophe Living, Using the Wisdom of Your Body and Mind to Face Stress, Pain and Illness, (New York: Random House, September 24, 2013, Revised Edition)

[12] Dr. Kathy J. Forti, "Trinfinity8," Trinfinity and Beyond, http://trinfinity8.com/blog (accessed April 12, 2012)

[13] Bentinho Massaro, Free Online School for Enlightenment and Empowerment http://trinfinityacademy.com

[14] Ibid

Acknowledgments

My husband Kevin, thank you for always supporting my dreams, no matter how crazy they are, and for loving me with a love not of this world. Going through all the waves of emotion as I was writing this book, you rode them with me, and not once did you threaten to strangle me. That is a testament to how truly blessed I am to share my life with you. You are my home, baby!

Bentinho Massaro, your Foreword is brilliant; thank you so much for writing it. I am beyond grateful for finally having all the pieces of the puzzle, and that is thanks to you and everything you are. Oh, and by the way, I had never heard of "eye gazing" until I attended your retreat in Sedona.

Dr. Besemann, we lived this crazy journey together and I couldn't be more grateful to you. You are not only an extraordinary human being, but a once in a lifetime physician. Thank you for writing the beautiful Introduction. I am honored to call you my friend.

To everyone at NutriChem, there truly are no words to express my gratitude for you. You are beyond phenomenal, and each and every one of you has a piece of my heart. I hope you know the difference you are making in peoples' lives, every single day.

Kent MacLeod, the founder of NutriChem, what could I possibly say to the man who brought me back to life? To the man who didn't just walk away from a palliative patient, but rolled up his sleeves and got to work. "Thank you" just doesn't cover it, Kent. I will love you always and forever. Keep doing you Kent, making people happy and healthy.

Dr. Joyce Buckley, your words of wisdom have carried me through some of the toughest times in my life. Had it not been for you keeping me not only alive, but thriving for all of these years, I wouldn't now have the privilege of being Mom's caregiver. I am beyond grateful for your care, your love and your integrity. You truly are the best of the best.

Marie Goutière, my friend and sister from another mother, thank you for contributing to this book in a massive way and for being you.

Janet Marchant, thank you for reading the manuscript repeatedly, motivating me, and guiding me on how this book had to be structured. Thank you for holding my hand when I needed it the most. Janet chose the three part titles, "Hell, Heaven and Here" to help me divide the book into sections. I love you, Janet, and I am eternally grateful for you.

Lisa Rapp, what would have happened had it not been for you? The book was being uploaded for publishing, and you implored me to stop the presses. And thank heavens. Here I thought you needed to read the book immediately because you just couldn't wait for it to be published. Little did I know the book needed you! Lisa completely re-edited this book in its entirety out of the goodness of her heart. She told me this book deserved to read beautifully and that's exactly what she's done. There are no words to express my love and gratitude for you Lisa. Thank you.

And last but not least, my publisher and friend, Carol, you rock! Thank you for repeatedly kicking me in the ass to get this book finished. I did it, beauty!

Tina Blackwell found her purpose and her passion when she decided to use her traumatic experiences and her unwavering strength to overcome them by helping others who may feel defeated by similar life and death situations.

Tina broke all classic medical assumptions with her health battles. Told she would be disabled permanently, she not only proved them wrong, she overcame PTSD, chronic pain, narcotic dependency and physical disabilities.

A debilitating accident led her to be a seeker of life's meaning and truth, which she now shares as a motivational speaker. Tina's mission is physical, emotional and spiritual healing for all.

Tina currently lives in Ottawa, Canada with her two life-long champions, her mother Polline and her husband Kevin. Oh, and her precious dog, Willow.